I0480193

ART BOOKS

FROM CRESCENT MOON PUBLISHING

Leonardo da Vinci
by James Pearson

Early Netherlandish Painting
by Rosalind Mutter

Piero della Francesca
by Naomi Haskell

Giovanni Bellini
by Julia Davis

Eric Gill: Nuptials of God
by Anthony Hoyland

Minimal Art and Artists In the 1960s and After
by Laura Garrard

Postwar Art
by George Knighton

Vincent van Gogh: Visionary Landscapes
by Stuart Morris

Max Beckmann
by Stuart Morris

Egon Schiele: Sex and Death in Purple Stockings
by D. Simon Eade

Mark Rothko: The Art of Transcendence
by Julia Davis

Jasper Johns
by L.M. Poole

Brice Marden
by Laura Garrard

Frank Stella: American Abstract Artist
by James Pearson

FRA ANGELICO

Fra Angelico

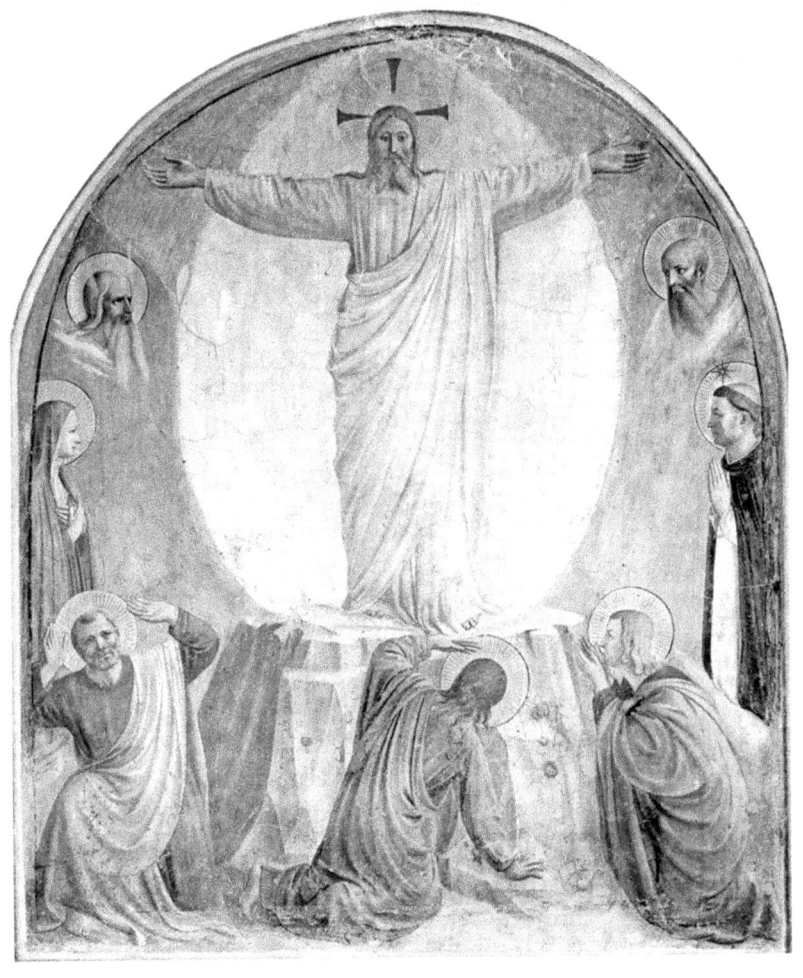

J.B. SUPINO

TRANSLATED BY LEADER SCOTT

Crescent Moon

First published 1902. This edition © 2017.

Printed and bound in the U.S.A.
Set in Book Antiqua 10 on 14pt.
Designed by Radiance Graphics.

Thanks to the authors and publishers quoted.

British Library Cataloguing in Publication data

ISBN-13 9781861716026 (Pbk)

CRESCENT MOON PUBLISHING
P.O. Box 1312, Maidstone, Kent, ME14 5XU
Great Britain, www.crmoon.com

CONTENTS

NOTE ON THE TEXT

Fra Angelico by J.B. Supino, translated by Leader Scott, and published by Allinari, Florence, 1902.

The illustrations discussed in the book are included in the illustrations section, along with many other works.

Footnotes are in square brackets, thus: [*1].

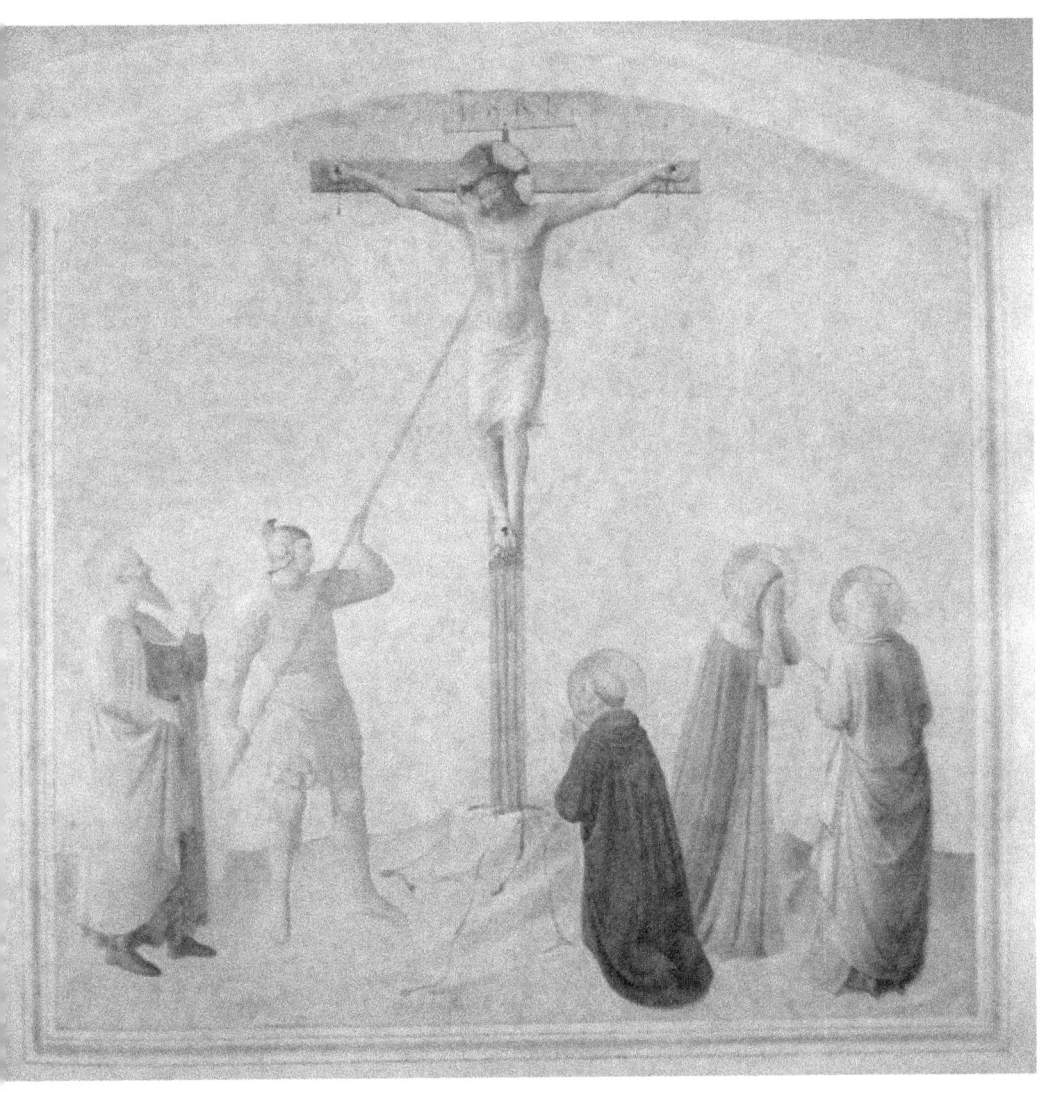

Fra Angelico, Crucifixion, cell 42, San Marco

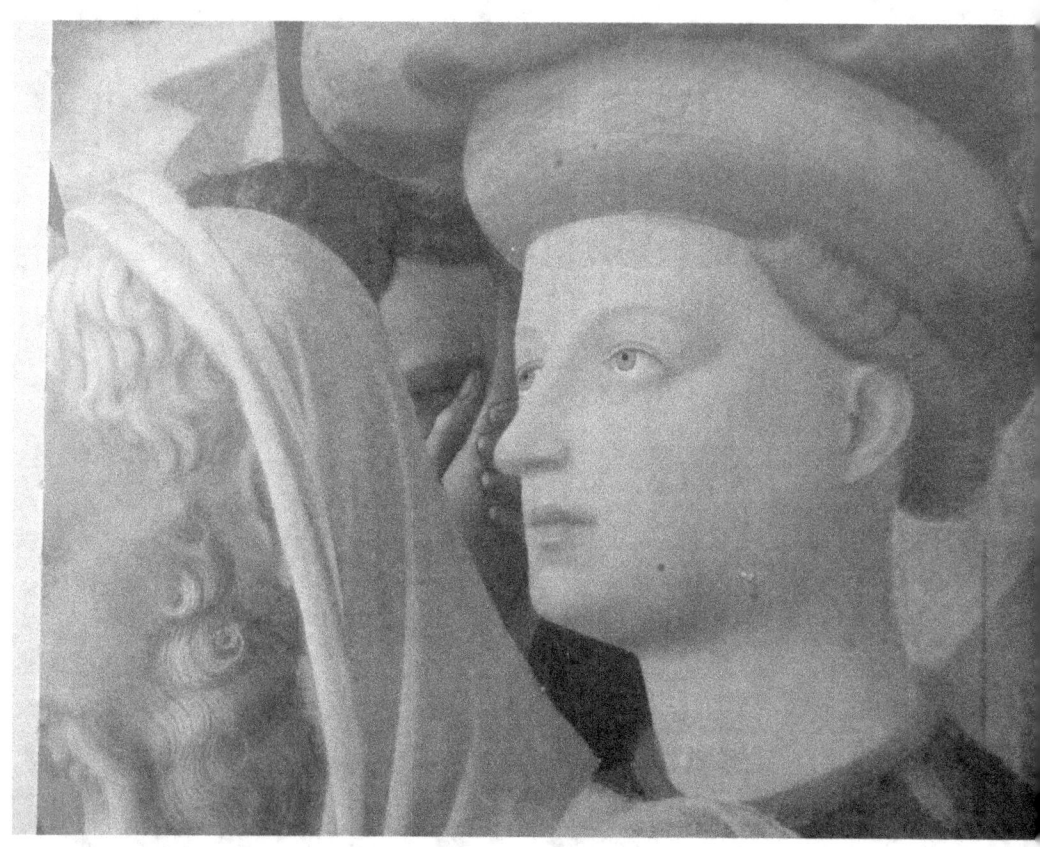

Fra Angelico, Descent From the Cross, detail, San Marco

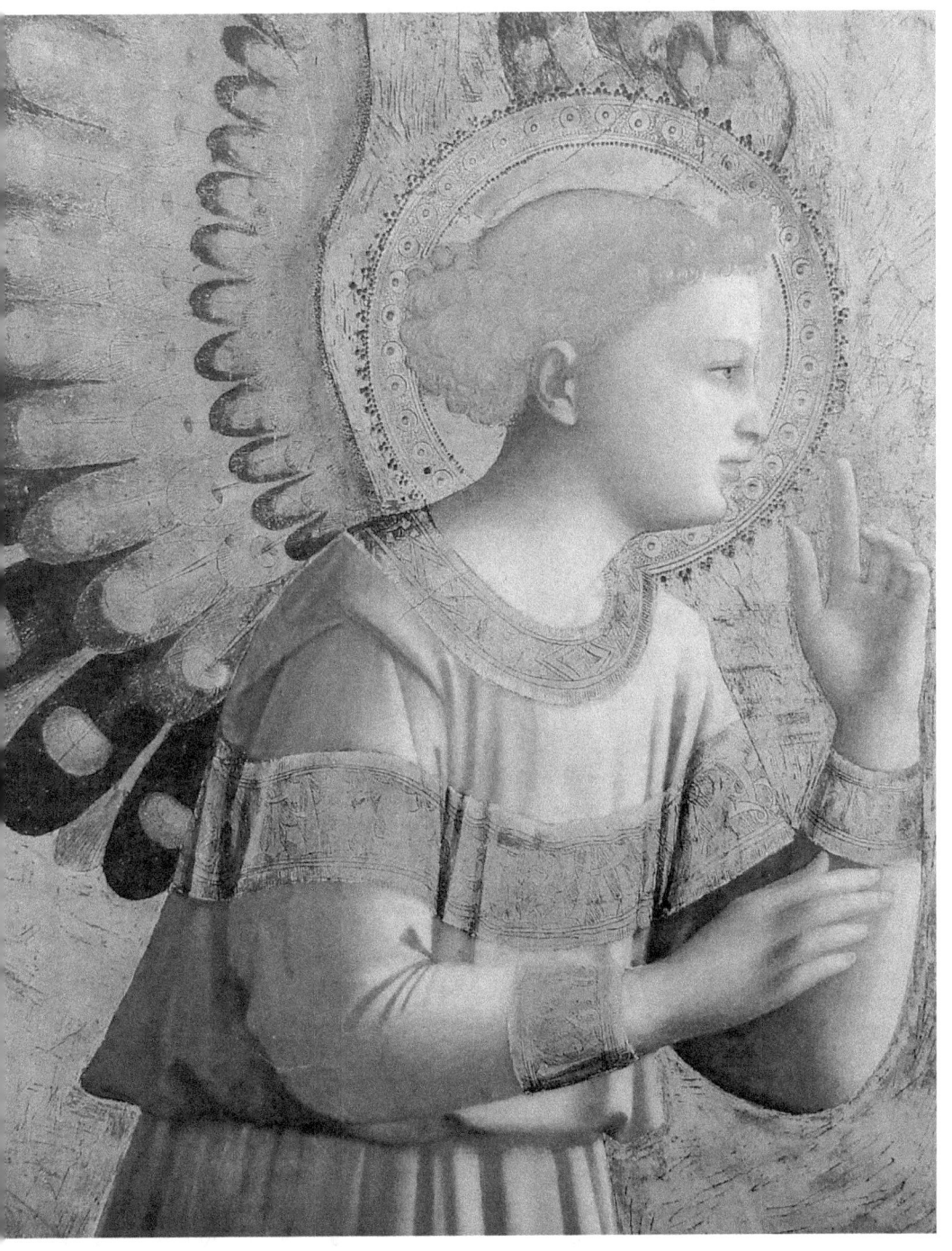

Fra Angelico, Annunciatory Angel, c. 1437-46, Detroit Institute of Arts

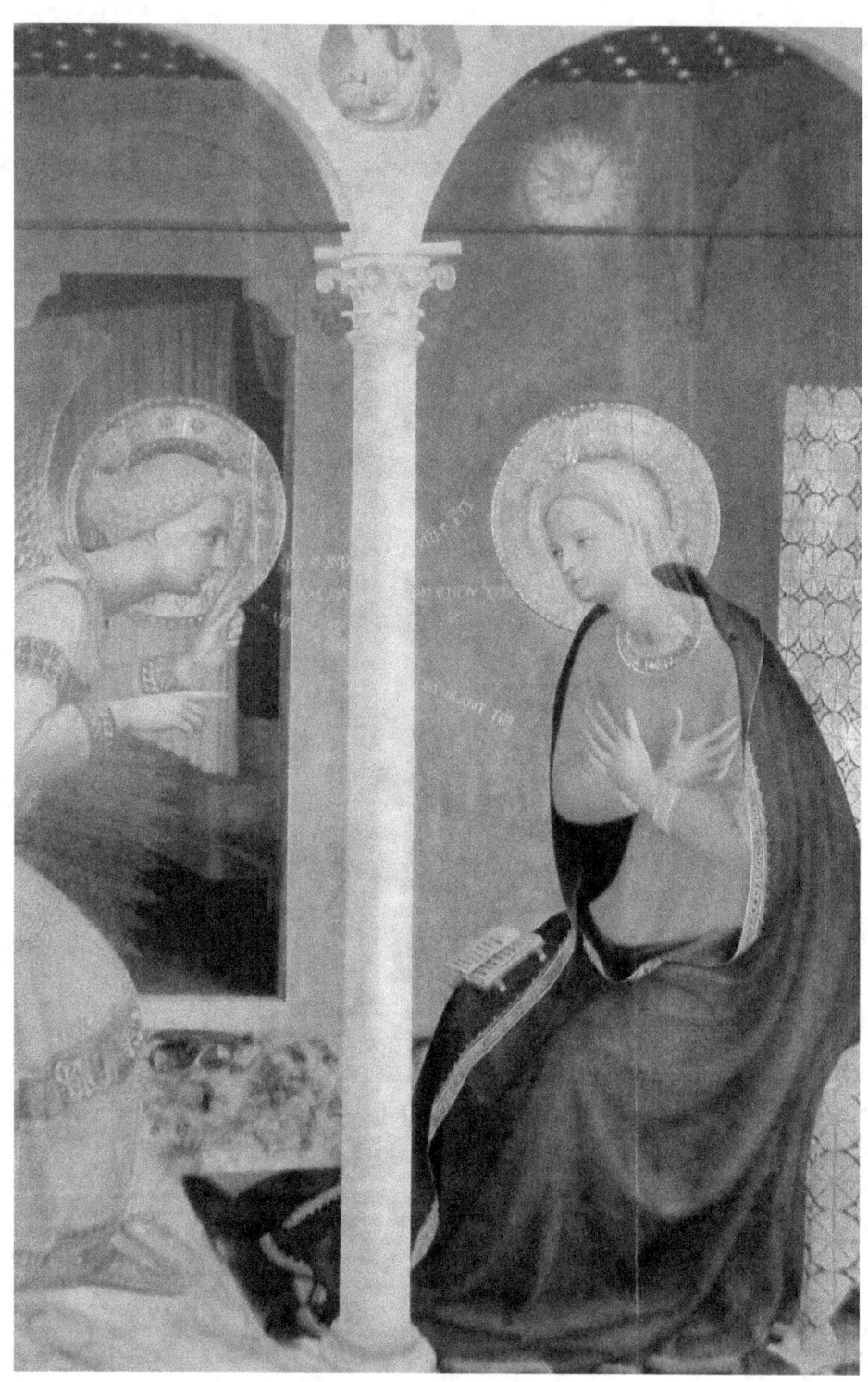

Fra Angelico, Anunciation, Cortona

PROEM – BEATO ANGELICO

Tradition shows us Fra Giovanni Angelico absorbed in his work, and either caressing with his brush one of those graceful angelic figures which have made him immortal, or reverently outlining the sweet image of the Virgin before which he himself would kneel in adoration. Legend pictures him devoutly prostrate in prayer before commencing work, that his soul might be purified, and fitted to understand and render the divine subject; and again in oration after leaving his easel, to thank heaven for having given him power to make his holy visions visible to other eyes.

But has tradition any foundation in fact? Why not? Through his numberless works we may easily divine the soul of the artist, and can well understand, how the calm and serene atmosphere of the monastic cell, the church perfumed with incense, and the cloister vibrating with psalms, would develop the mystic sentiment in such a mind.

And can we disregard tradition in face of such humility of life, such beauty of work, exquisite refinement of feeling, and sweetness of expression!

Among all the masters who have attempted to imbue the human form with the divine spirit, he is perhaps the only one who succeeded in producing pure celestial figures, and this with such marvellous simplicity of line, that they have become the glory of his art.

Whether it be the Virgin enthroned amidst groups of cherubim sounding heavenly trumpets, or Christ blessing the just and driving away sinners; whether the martyrs supporting their torments with superhuman resignation, the apostles preaching the gospel, or angels free in the air and chanting celestial glories; the same spirit is in them all – at once intense, devout, and utterly pure, in which the fervent believer and the true artist are inseparably blended.

The reason is, that Fra Giovanni put into his work the flame of an overpowering passion; under his touch features were beautified, and figures animated with a new mystic grace. He threw himself entirely into his art which thus became the spontaneous expression of his soul. "It was the custom of Fra Giovanni," says Vasari, "to abstain from retouching or improving any painting once finished. He altered nothing, but left all as it was done the first time, believing, as he said, that such was the will of God. It is also affirmed that he would never take his pencil in hand until he had first offered a prayer. He is said never to have painted a crucifix without tears streaming from his eyes, and in the countenances and attitudes of his figures it is easy to perceive proof of his sincerity, his goodness, and the depth of his devotion to the religion of Christ."[*1]

How this devout mind, full of the figurative sacred writings then current, must have overflowed with visions, ecstasies and miracles! And what tremors of awe must he have felt, in putting these visions into colour! His Madonnas, their features suffused with candour and humility, bend with maternal grace hitherto unwitnessed, in loving contemplation of the Son, or – mothers in glory – they bow to receive the homage of the Redeemer. His saints ecstatically gaze at luminous celestial apparitions; his golden winged angels dance lightly beneath the throne of their Lord or sound merrily the most various instruments, singing: *laudate Dominum..., laudate eum in sono tubæ, laudate eum in psalterio et cithara, laudate eum in timpano et choro...*; or else with their fair curly heads downcast they reverently worship the divine majesty. What a feast of light and colour is in these panels, gleaming with azure and gold like a hymn to religion and faith!

> "We know from him how the pious imagination of the men of his time pictured the Kingdom of Heaven, with the angels, saints, and blessed ones, and on this account alone his pictures would have been of extraordinary importance in the history of religion. Not to love Fra Angelico would mean to lack the true sentiment of ancient art, for though we recognize the pious *naïveté* of the monk, there is in the heavenly beauty of his figures, and the joy of youthful faith which animates the artist, a charm unequalled in the whole history of Art!"[*2]

Whether Fra Angelico ever actually had a master, it is impossible to ascertain. There are critics who affirm that if anyone initiated him in art, imbuing him with his own sentiment and style, it might have been the Camaldolese monk Lorenzo Monaco; but Cavalcaselle justly observes that between Angelico and Lorenzo Monaco there only exists that affinity which in coetaneous artists results from community of thought, social conditions, and religious sentiments. Two monks like the Camaldolese and the Dominican might well show the same ideas, without implying a relation of master and scholar between them.[*3]

Both critics and historians, however, agree in the assertion that he began his career in art by illuminating codices and choral books. Baldinucci and Rosini judge that his master in painting was the Florentine Gherardo Starnina, whom Lanzi designates as "a painter of life-like style." But Padre Marchese refuting this opinion observes that "not to mention Vasari's silence on the matter, the fact is very doubtful, because Gherardo passed many years in Spain, and returning to his native land died in 1403, when little Guido of Mugello"[*4] was only 16 years old, an age which scarcely admits of the first steps in Art.[*5] But the date of Starnina's death is now corrected and proved to have been in 1408, so, taking into account the character of our artist's works, nothing need now be opposed to the theory that Fra Giovanni may have profited by the teaching of that master, while living in

Florence after his return from Spain; besides it is not proved whether that journey to Spain was ever really taken. Historians, it is true, tell us that Starnina, being obliged to leave Florence after the Ciompi riots (1378), took refuge in Spain, where he lived several years; but it is certain that in 1387 his name was inscribed in the Guild of Florentine painters.[*6]

Vasari does not doubt that Fra Angelico, like other artists from Masaccio onwards, acquired his skill by studying the frescoes of the Brancacci Chapel;[*7] but besides the fact that the style of those pictures is diametrically opposed to Fra Angelico's, the latter could not possibly have been in Masaccio's school, for as he was born in 1387, he was fifteen years older than Masaccio and already a proved master, when the Carmine frescoes were being painted. Fra Angelico's style is so individual and characteristic, that it might rather be considered as springing from his own disposition, developed under the influence of his time. Studying the works left in Florence by his great predecessors, leading a retired life, and purifying every idea, every inspiration in the fire of religion, Angelico was enabled, by meditation, to perfect the models of the best artists of the "trecento", among whom we should opine that the influence of Orcagna in his frescoes in the Strozzi Chapel of S. M. Novella, was greater even than that of Giotto. Indeed it is evident that what Orcagna began, is carried to the highest development in Fra Angelico, who combined softness and refinement with severity of form, grace of expression with nobility of attitude.

The figure of the Virgin in the fresco of the Judgment in the Strozzi Chapel, so grand and majestic in its simplicity, is again recognisable in the panels of Fra Angelico, imitated with his own especial character and spiritual feeling, full of grace and humility, the soft lines breathing beauty and lightness. The saints who appear to be actually in celestial repose, have also inspired Fra Giovanni; the same gentle and contemplative expression which irradiates the features of the elect is again visible in our painter's figures. In the colouring of both, vivacity is combined with softness, and vigour of chiaro-scuro goes together with transparency of tint.

Nevertheless it is true that in certain respects, Fra Angelico might be said to belong to the same school as Masolino. They are, however, at the antipodes from each other in sentiment and artistic interpretation, for while the saintly Giovanni endeavoured to idealize the human figure and render it divine, Masolino, like most of his contemporaries, followed a style distinctly realistic; yet it may be proved that in technique, both followed the same rules, and worked on similar principles. In fact the similitude between the two painters noticeable in their composition, softness of outline, lightness of figures, and clear harmonious colouring, tends to confirm the great artistic affinity which we have indicated. Both of them used rosy tints in the flesh, with greenish and yellowish shadows, both recall the older artists of the "trecento" in the perspective, which is often incorrect, and out of proportion. But how far superior is Fra Angelico when the work of both in its full aspect is compared!

•

Fra Angelico has, it is true, conventional forms, and there is a certain sameness in his heads with their large oval countenances; the small eyes, outlined round the upper arch of the eyebrow, and with a black spot for pupils, sometimes lack expression, or have a too monotonous one, and the iris is often lost in the white of the cornea; his mouths are always drawn small with a thickening of the lips in the centre, and the corners strongly accentuated; the colour of his faces is either too pink or too yellow; the folds of the robes (often independent of the figure, especially in the lower part) fall straight, and in the representations of the seated Virgin expand on the ground, as if to form the foot of a chalice. But in his frescoes these faults of conventional manner almost entirely disappear, giving place to freer drawing, more life-like expression, and a character of greater power.

We will not repeat with Vasari that Fra Giovanni perfected his art from the frescoes of the Brancacci Chapel; but we do not doubt that he too felt the beneficent influx of the new style, of which Masaccio was the greatest champion, and that he followed it, leaving behind, up to a certain point, the primitive Giottesque forms. There is in his art, the great mediæval ideal rejuvenated and reinvigorated by the spirit of newer times. Being in the beginning of his career, as is generally believed, only an illuminator, he continued, with subtle delicacy and accurate, almost timid design, to illuminate in larger proportions on his panels, those figures which are often only parts of a decorative whole. But in his later works while still preserving the simplicity of handling, and the innate character of his style, he displays a new tendency, and learns to give life to his figures, not only by the expression of purity and sweet ecstasy, but in finer particularization of form and action which he reproduces in more material style.

His clear diaphanous transparency of colouring is not used from lack of technical ability, but to approach more nearly to his ideal of celestial and divine visions, and succeed in a species of pictorial religious symbolism.

In the midst of his calm and serene compositions Fra Angelico has figures in which a healthy realism is strongly accentuated; figures drawn with decision, strong chiaro-scuro and robust colouring, which show that he did not deliberately disdain the progress made in art by his contemporaries. Indeed we should err in believing that Fra Angelico was unwilling to recognize the artistic developments going on around him, and the new tendencies followed by his eminent neighbours Ghiberti, Brunelleschi and Donatello. It was not so; but he only profited by the movement as far as he deemed possible without losing his own sentiment and character; thus giving a rare example of self-knowledge.

Perhaps he divined that if he had followed the new current too closely, it would have carried him farther than he wished to go; that the new manner would have removed him for ever from his ideal; in a word, that too intense study of the real, would have

diminished or entirely impeded fantasy and feeling. He instinct-
ively saw these perils, and therefore kept himself constant to his
old style, and while perfecting himself in it, he still remained
what he always had been, and what he felt he should be.

Though constrained to repeat to excess the usual subjects, too
traditionally drawn, "he often," as Burckhardt writes, "understood
how to avoid in the features of his saintly personages that aspect
of abstract impersonality, which had hitherto marked them, and
to animate them with delicate and individual life. He succeeded
in giving a new character to the time-honoured types used in
preceding artistic representations. To prove this it is sufficient to
cite the St. John Baptist – one of Fra Angelico's finest creations.

He modifies the traditional type of Christ according to his own
faith and feeling. Deriving it from Giotto, with improvements
gathered from Orcagna, he excels both masters, impressing on it a
divine character, and giving to the face of the Man God a sweet
gentleness which is truly sublime. These qualities reach the
highest grade in the "Coronation of the Virgin" at the Convent of
San Marco, and in the picture at Pisa[*8] where the Saviour is
represented standing upright, in the act of blessing with his right
hand, while in the uplifted left he holds a golden cup.

He is represented full face, in all his majesty, his features of
an exquisite sweetness and nobility, – a grand figure, which has
all the seduction of a vision, such as our Dominican alone could
conceive and design.

As he could, in a manner no one had ever done before, give
to the figure of the living Christ the expression of infinite
goodness, ready for sacrifice; so in his Crucifixions, instead of
following the example of his contemporaries, who depicted Christ
already dead, with marks of sorrow on His features, and contorted
by the spasm of a violent death; he represented Him living, calm
and serene, conscious of the sacrifice He completed, and full of joy
in dying for man's salvation.

The type of the Virgin, too, though its characteristic con-
struction of features, and short and receding chin, are derived

from the Sienese masters, especially from Lorenzetti, in Fra Angelico responds to an artistic idealization chosen by him as approaching more the divinity of her person. The flowing robes of the Virgin show her long and refined hands, but beneath that mantle he draws no feminine figure nor can one even guess at it. All the power of the artist is concentrated in her face

umile in tanta gloria,
(humble in such great glory)

on which the artist has impressed such candour, and so lively an expression of ineffable grace, that one is involuntarily moved to devotion.

The divine child with its golden curls, full and sunny face, wide open and sparkling eyes, is in the pictures at Cortona and Perugia depicted with rosy fingers in the act of blessing; in the "Madonna della Stella" He embraces His mother so closely that He almost hides Himself in her bosom; in the great azure-surrounded tabernacle of the Linen Guild, He is smiling; while in the fresco of the corridor at San Marco, He has an ingenuous wondering gaze as He holds forth His little hand, – an expression so natural that it shows a happy grafting of ideal representation, on a conscientious and close study of the real.

Full of character, too, are the heads of his old people, with flowing beards and severe aspect, and those of his saints and martyrs, which were evidently either young novices of the convent, contemporary brethren, or elder companions in the faith, portrayed with sapient and ingenuous realism. But the figures which most brilliantly display his genius, are those diaphanous angels, robed in flowing tunics, resplendent with gold, and of infinite variety. While admiring that multitude of celestial creatures, who praise, sing and dance around the radiant Madonnas, how can we doubt that they have visited his cell, and that he has lived with them in a fraternal and sweet familiarity?[*9]

•

Even when he has to represent scenes of passion, Fra Angelico mitigates the violence of action with softness of sentiment, for anger and disdain never entered his soul; and in their place he prefers to reproduce one character alone in all his figures with their gentle expression. It is his own character, with its angelic goodness of heart, which he incarnates in the divine beauty of all these celestial beings. As in name and art, so in real life he was truly "angelic," for he spent his whole time in the service of God, and the good of his neighbour and the world.

"And what more can or ought to be desired, than by thus living righteously," says Vasari, "to secure the kingdom of heaven, and by labouring virtuously, to obtain everlasting fame in this world? And, of a truth, so extraordinary and sublime a gift as that possessed by Fra Giovanni, should scarcely be conferred on any but a man of most holy life, since it is certain that all who take upon them to meddle with sacred and ecclesiastical subjects, should be men of holy and spiritual minds...

"Fra Giovanni was a man of the utmost simplicity of intention, and was most holy in every act of his life... He disregarded all earthly advantages; and, living in pure holiness, was as much the friend of the poor in life as I believe his soul now is in heaven. He laboured continually at his paintings, but would do nothing that was unconnected with things holy. He might have been rich, but for riches he took no care; on the contrary, he was accustomed to say, that the only true riches was contentment with little. He might have commanded many, but would not do so, declaring that there was less fatigue and less danger of error in obeying others, than in command-ing others. It was at his option to hold places of dignity in the brotherhood of his Order, and also in the world; but he regarded them not, affirming that he sought no dignity and took no care but that of escaping hell and drawing near to Paradise. And, of a truth, what dignity can be compared to that which should be most coveted by all churchmen, nay, by every man living, that, namely, which is found in God alone, and in a life of virtuous labour?

"Fra Giovanni was kindly to all, and moderate in all his habits, living temperately, and holding himself entirely apart from the snares of the world. He used frequently to say, that he who practised the art of painting had need of quiet, and should live without cares or anxious thoughts; adding, that he who would do the work of Christ should perpetually remain with Christ. He was never seen to display anger among the brethren of his order; a thing which appears to me most extraordinary, nay, almost incredible; if he admonished his friends, it was with gentleness and a quiet smile; and to those who sought his works, he would reply with the utmost cordiality, that they had but to obtain the assent of the prior, when he would assuredly not fail to do what they desired. In fine, this never-sufficiently-to-be-lauded father was most humble, modest, and excellent in all his words and works; in his painting he gave evidence of piety and devotion, as well as of ability, and the saints that he painted have more the air and expression of sanctity than have those of any other master." [*10]

•

Fra Giovanni Angelico, whose worldly name was Guido or Guidolino (little Guy), was born in the year 1387; his father was named Piero (surname not known) of Vicchio in the Mugello; – that pleasant valley which boasts of having given birth to Giotto.

Vasari asserts that Guido's brother Benedetto, a miniaturist, was also very clever in a larger style of painting, but the researches of Milanesi quite refute this opinion, and show that Benedetto did nothing more than copy choral books, and that he continued this kind of work till his death.[*11]

"The most ancient chronicles of the convent of St. Mark and St. Dominic at Fiesole," writes Milanesi when registering the death of Fra Benedetto brother of Angelico, in the year 1448, "remark simply that he was a very good writer, and that he wrote and annotated the choral books of St. Mark and some of those of St. Dominic." We have only the evidence in Vasari and the "Annali del Convento di San Marco," written after his Lives of the Painters to prove that he was a miniaturist.[*12]

In these Annals it is added, with more historical truth, that although Angelico "might have conveniently lived in the world, and besides his own possessions might have gained any income he chose, with the art for which he was famous even in his youth, yet, for his own satisfaction and peace, being by nature steady and good, and chiefly also for the salvation of his soul he preferred to take the vows in the order of the Preaching monks."[*13] This happened in 1407.

On the slopes of the smiling hill of Fiesole the foundations of a new convent were being laid by Giovanni Dominici, the great preacher and reformer, who wished in this new monastery to give a model to all the cloistered orders which at the close of the preceding century had greatly fallen from their ancient observances. St. Antonino was among the first to embrace this reform, and after two years Guidolino and his brother followed his example, choosing the robes of St. Dominic.

On being received by the Dominicans they were sent to Cortona, where St. Antonino and others already resided, there being as yet no novitiate at the Fiesole convent. In 1408 they took the irrevocable vows, but it cannot be ascertained whether they still remained at Cortona, or returned at once to their own convent at Fiesole. If the latter, the two brothers must have been involved in the vicissitudes of the Fiesolan convent, which, refusing to acknowledge Pope Alexander V. (who was elected by the Council of Pisa 1409), entered into a fierce contest with the archbishop of Florence. The convent was abandoned by its inmates who fled to Foligno to avoid the rule of Fra Tommaso da Fermo, General of the Order, who had sworn obedience to the new Pope. They were received as guests at Foligno by Ugolino de' Trinci, lord of the city, and Federigo Frezzi, author of the *Quadriregio*. Here they passed five years, being treated with great benevolence by their brethren, nor did they leave until driven away by the plague in 1414, when they again took shelter at Cortona where they remained till 1418.

•

When Guidolino entered the convent and took the name of Giovanni, he must have been already expert in art; for the vicissitudes which followed could certainly not have facilitated the study of painting. In fact his works which remain at Cortona are in so youthful a style, and bear the imprint of such freshness as to remove all doubt on this generally accepted assertion.

While staying at Foligno, the Fiesolan refugees propagated

that severe form of life and strict observance which Giovanni Dominici had taught in his convent at Fiesole, and brother Giovanni again began his artistic work, for painting was to him like prayer, i.e. his usual way of raising his mind and heart to God. Unfortunately few of these first works have been preserved, but from those few we are assured that he studied in Florence, from which school alone he could have appropriated the noble manner impressed on all his works; and that those who perceive an Umbrian influence in his art, are very far from the truth.

There may be some elements common to both the Umbrian art and that of Angelico; this, however, does not depend so much on the teaching of the school, as on technical affinity; insomuch as Umbrian painting in its lucidity, charm and accuracy of colour, is in some measure derived from the art of illumination, and most probably Fra Angelico took his style from the same source, as even in his most perfect works, he always preserved a remembrance of it.

In fact, his patient diligence and study of detail render his pictures so many miniatures, done in larger proportions; the lucidity of tint, the grace of the ornamental motives, the almost exaggerated minuteness of execution, are decided proofs of the artistic education of Fra Angelico. It is pleasant to imagine him, during his sojourn at Foligno and Cortona, making pilgrimages to Assisi, to draw inspiration from the works of the great masters in the splendid church of San Francesco. There he found his old friends, and might at a glance admire together Giotto, Simone Martini, and Lorenzetto. We should say he admired Simone and Lorenzetto more than Giotto, for the grace of their figures, refinement of execution, and greater richness of the accessories, robes and ornamentation, together with the pleasing brilliance of colouring, all approached more nearly to Fra Giovanni's own artistic sentiment than the style of Giotto.

And even less than the Umbrian painters or miniaturists (if indeed there were any worthy to influence the artistic spirit of our artist) did the landscape of verdant Umbria stir his soul, which even the sweet slopes of Fiesole could not touch.

Doubtless from the heights of the convent at Cortona, which dominates one of the finest views in Italy, the young monk admired the beautiful horizon, and enjoyed the splendour of the verdant plain, and the blue mountains, "enwrapt in mists of purple and gold", as he had often at sunrise and sunset, enjoyed from his Fiesole convent the gentle fields and dales "peopled with houses and olives"; but, after all, these beauties of nature so often displayed before him, were dumb to an artist who was wholly absorbed in visions beyond this world.

The study of the verdant country never occupied his mind; in his paintings, landscape is either an insignificant accessory, or if it occupies a large space in the picture as in the "Deposition from the Cross" in the Florentine Gallery, it shows plainly that it is not the result of special study, of personal impressions, or of love of the place itself. In fact it does not attract or interest the observer at all.

Nor could this be otherwise; the inner life of the spirit, which he lived so intensely, and so vividly transfused in the figures of his Saints, must necessarily have abstracted his mind from his surroundings, to which he therefore gave little attention. In this he was faithful to the Giottesque principle of not enriching the background, except by just what was necessary to render the subject intelligible, and this without pretension, or new research.

His trees rose straight on their trunks, the leaves and branches spreading in conventional style; his rocks have the usual gradations which we find in the old school; the views of distant cities are absolutely fantastic and infantile creations; only the green plain is often illumined, in an unusual manner, by tiny flowerets of many hues, while mystic roses crown the angels' locks, adorn overflowing baskets, or rise on long stalks at the foot of the Virgin's throne in transparent vases.

Such are the characteristics, the spirit and the sentiment that appear in the works of Fra Angelico, who might be considered as the last representative of that school of which Giotto was master;

and at the same time the initiator of "Quattrocento" art, whose powerful development irresistibly attracted him. He painted so many pictures for the houses of Florentine citizens, that "I was often astonished," writes Vasari, "how one man alone could, even in many years, do so much and so well." "And we also," justly observes Milanesi, "are not less amazed than Vasari, for although many works have been dispersed or are still hidden, yet a great number still remain both in Italy and other countries, and, what is more remarkable, the greater part are not mentioned by Vasari."[*14]

We will follow our artist in his different places of abode, thus establishing the various periods of his life and artistic productions; from the Fiesole hills, where the first seedlings of his fantasy were sown, to green Umbria, where his early works are, works warm with enthusiasm, faith and youthful candour: from Florence, which he enriched with admirable frescoes, and innumerable pictures dazzling with gold and azure, to Rome, where he left his grand pictorial legacy in the oratory of Pope Nicholas V.

I

FRA ANGELICO

AT CORTONA AND PERUGIA

[1409-1418]

If, after a study of the pictorial works of Fra Angelico, any one should undertake to make a precise classification of them, he would – although his frescoes are easy enough to classify – find himself confronted by no small difficulty in regard to the panel paintings.

So active and original was the artist, and so grand in his simplicity, that he always remained just what he appeared from the beginning, – the painter of ingenuous piety, mystical ecstasy, and intense religious fervour.

No record is extant of his first visit to Foligno, but in the church of St. Dominic at Cortona we may still admire a triptych with the Virgin and four Saints; an Annunciation; and two "predelle"; one of which is said to have belonged to the picture of St. Dominic, as the scenes relate to the life of that Saint, and the other with some stories of the Virgin, to the Annunciation mentioned above.

To the story of St. Dominic (which had already been treated in a masterly manner by Fra Guglielmo, in the "arca" at Bologna, and by Traini in his picture at Pisa), Fra Angelico has, in some scenes, given a fuller development, but with less dramatic sentiment; exactly the good and bad points which are more clearly shown in his other works. The "predella", divided into seven parts, represents the birth of Saint Dominic; the dream of Pope Honorius III., to whom the Saint appears in act of steadying the falling church; the meeting of the Saint with St. Francis; the confirmation of his rule by means of the Virgin; the visits of St. Peter and St. Paul; the dispute with heretics; the resurrection of the nephew of Cardinal de' Ceccani; the supper of the Saint and his brethren; and lastly his death.

The scene of the resurrection of the young Napoleon, nephew of Cardinal Stefano de' Ceccani, had been already powerfully depicted by Traini; in Angelico's hands it comes out restrained and cold, the acts of amazement in the devotees present at the miracle, who raise their hands in astonishment, are too conventional: and it is precisely in the intermingling of these gestures of sorrow for the death, and wonder for the revivication, that the Pisan artist has brought out his best effects. As we have before pointed out, the calm spirit of Fra Angelico avoided realistic representation; his figures always suggest love, faith and resignation, but are never agitated; like the soul of their author, they are incapable of violent action; therefore when these should be drawn, the representation falls below reality. We shall see instances of this in other works of his.

•

One of Angelico's most familiar subjects was the Annunciation, and the most interesting of the Cortona pictures, is that of the angel's visit to Mary. Its motive is simple and clear, as it was transmitted from early Christian art; the general lines are unchanged, but the expression greatly so. Fra Angelico did not disturb the religious solemnity of the apparition with useless accessories; faithful to his own sentiment, he has clothed Mary with humility. She sits beneath the portico, the book neglected on her lap, her hands crossed, and her drooping head inclined towards the heavenly messenger. The golden-winged angel with roseate robe also bends before the Virgin, the right hand pointing to her breast and the left to the dove which sheds celestial rays on Mary's head. In the background Adam and Eve are being expelled from the terrestrial Paradise, symbol of the ancient Christian legend which directly connects the story of original sin with that of the Redemption.

This mystic subject, which does not lack grace and freshness in the Cortona painting, finds its fuller development in San Marco at Florence. Here the Madonna is seated on a wooden stool, her head projected forward almost in ecstasy, with hands clasped on her breast, and in similar attitude the angel half kneels before her. The scene takes place before a little grated window in the colonnade of a cloister, utterly bare of ornament, but in this very simplicity lies all the charm and poetry of Angelico.

Before a subject so ideal, so solemn, which reveals in such intensity of faith and feeling how his thought spontaneously turned to the prayer of the Salutation which was certainly on the artist's lips as he painted, or was inspired by some sweet Annunciation hymn such as this, which probably has been often repeated before this entrancing picture:

Alzando gli occhi vidi Maria bella
Col libro in mano, e l' angel gli favella.

Dinnanzi a lei si stava inginocchiato
Quell' angel Gabriel tanto lucente,
Ed umilmente a lei ebbe parlato:
"Vergine pura, non temer niente;
Messaggio son di Dio onnipotente,
Che t' ha eletta e vuolti per sua sposa."

E poi le disse: "In cielo è ordinato,

Che siate madre del figliuol di Dio,
Però che gli angeli il padre han pregato,
Che con effetto adempia el lor disio;
E da parte del sommo e buono Dio,
Questa benedizione a voi s' appella."

Queste parole fur tanto infiammate
E circundate di virtù d' amore,
Che ben parean da Dio fussin mandate,
E molto se n' allegra nel suo core:
"Da poi che piace all' alto Dio Signore,
Io son contenta d' essere sua ancella."

Ella si stava dentro alla sua cella,
E grande meraviglia si faceva,
Però che a nessun uomo ella favella,
E molto timorosa rispondeva.
L' angelo disse allora: "Ave Maria,
Di grazia tu se' piena, o chiara stella."

Allor discese lo Spirito santo,
Come un razzo di sol l' ha circundata,
Poi dentro a lei entrò quel frutto santo
In quella sacrestia chiusa e serrata;
Di poi partori inviolata
E si rimase vergine e donzella.

O veri amanti, venite a costei,
Quella che di bellezza è madonna:
L' aria e la terra si sostien per lei,
Del ciel regina e del mondo colonna,
Chi vuol veder la donzella gioconda
Vada a veder la nunziata bella.[*15]

The other predella at Cortona represents various episodes in the life of the Virgin:– the Nativity, Marriage, Visitation, Adoration of the Magi, Presentation in the Temple, Death, Burial and lastly the apparition of the Virgin to the blessed Dominican Reginald of Orleans. Padre Marchese believes that this last scene did not originally belong to the predella; but the doubt is unfounded, for nothing is more natural than the artist's wish to connect the history of the Virgin with his Order, of which she is the patroness.

Cavalcaselle, as well as Marchese, affirms that the scene of the Marriage of the Virgin reproduces that of the picture in the Uffizi at Florence. This may be, as far as the subject and scene go, but in the disposition of the figures, the development of action, the two works have nothing in common. Of course in both there must be the priest who unites the bridal couple, and around them the usual personages in various attitudes of complaisance, surprise, and rejoicing, but the grouping of the figures in the predella at Cortona is more naturally conceived. The women on the right appear to come from the house where they had met to assist at the ceremony; the men stand on the left. The background with its portico, and the walls, above which the trees of a garden project, are shown with more truth and solidity. To give wider scope to the scene Fra Angelico has depicted the marriage in an open space. The picture in the Uffizi, on the other hand, is so conventional both in architecture and landscape that it is impossible to establish a comparison between the two.

The Visitation depicts the wife of Zacharias meeting the Virgin, and lovingly embracing her; a serving maid leaning against the threshold, half hidden by the door, is listening with devotion, while another woman kneels on the ground in the road raising her hands to heaven.

In the Adoration of the Magi we find the usual qualities of composition and feeling. One of the Kings has already rendered homage to the Redeemer, and is talking to St. Joseph, who thanks him with earnest devotion; and while the second falls prone before the divine Child, and kisses His feet with profound emotion, the third prepares himself to render the required homage. All around are elegant little figures of pages and servants, in life-like and natural attitudes. The last story represents the Assumption of the Virgin, at which, according to ancient tradition, Christ is present and carries in his arms the soul of His mother in the form of a little child.

Padre Marchese wrote that both the Adoration and this

Assumption are in every respect similar, or replicas of those in the Uffizi. If anything, the pretty little panels of the Uffizi might be replicas of the Cortona ones; but in Florence the only painting with the scene of the Adoration of the Magi is that in the predella of the tabernacle of the Linen Weavers' Guild. Now, while the Adoration in the Cortona predella is naturally and simply pourtrayed, that of Florence is conventional and stiff, the vacuity of some figures and their actions is very evident – therefore this similitude also reduces itself to mere identity of subject. The Assumption of the Virgin also offers very notable differences. The predella at Cortona is more intense and severe, more simple and hence more grand; while the little panel in the Uffizi shows that the effort to embellish the scene has been too much for the artist, and the intensity of sentiment is greatly lessened, being injured by useless accessories. In that of Cortona, on the contrary, the figures of the Apostles who hold the sheet on which the Virgin reposes are full of expression and natural in action, the steep and mountainous background has severe and grand lines, as if to emphasize the sadness of the scene. Here the artist felt and created, there he merely repeated himself.

•

The triptych, once on the great altar of the church of San Domenico, now at a side altar on the right, has the Virgin seated in the centre with the Holy Child upright on her knee, his right hand is raised in act of benediction, and with his left he holds a rose. Around the throne are four angels, one of which carries a basket of flowers. In the side panels are St. Matthew, St. John Baptist, St. John the Evangelist and Mary Magdalene. Above in the central compartment of the triptych, is the Crucifixion and the two rounds on the sides represent the Annunciation.

In the Chapel of Sant' Orsola in San Domenico at Perugia there was formerly a panel picture now divided into many parts and much damaged. This was painted by Fra Giovanni for the Chapel of San Niccolò de' Guidalotti, and may now be seen in the Vannucci gallery at Perugia.

The Virgin is enthroned with her Son on her knees, His right hand in act of benediction, His left holding a half open pomegranate. At the foot of the throne four angels are standing back, the two first lift up a basket full of white and red roses, the others peep from behind the throne of the Virgin who turns lovingly to her little Son, who is entirely nude, and as rosy as the angels' flowers, and those in three vases at the foot of the throne. On the right of the Virgin are St. John Baptist and St. Catherine; on the left St. Dominic and St. Nicholas. On the predella, which is divided into three parts, were once various scenes from the life of St. Nicholas of Bari, two of these are now to be found in the Vatican Gallery. In a complex composition, they represent the birth of the Saint; his listening to the preaching of a bishop to a congregation of women seated in a flowery field; the Saint saving from dishonour the daughters of a poor gentleman; and the miracle of causing a hundred measures of wheat to rain down and relieve the famine in the city of Nuri. On the upper portion the Saint appears from behind a rock, having been invoked by some devotees to calm a tempest which threatened to wreck their bark.

•

The portion at Perugia represents the miraculous salvation of three innocent youths, sons of Roman princes; and the death and funeral of the Saint. In the lower part of the picture he is extended on the bier surrounded by monks, women and poor people who weep his loss, while above, his soul is being led to heaven by four angels. The frame of the painting is now divided into twelve fragments, each one containing a small figure of a Saint: they are St. Romuald, St. Gregory, St. Laurence, St. Bonaventure, St. Catherine, St. Peter Martyr, St. Mary Magdalene, St. Thomas Aquinas, St. Peter, St. Stephen, St. Paul and St. John. The last four figures have been mutilated in the lower part, and in these, as well as the others, the colouring is much injured. If it were desired to complete the altar-piece, at present, the gables of the tripartite frame would be missing, but there is no doubt that – as in the Cortona picture – the two small rounds in the Perugian

Pinacoteca, representing the Angel of the Annunciation and the Virgin, on gold backgrounds, formed part. Padre Marchese places this panel among the youthful works of the artist, "because it shows more than his other works the manner and technique of Giotto's school." Padre Timoteo Bottonio wrote that it was painted in 1437, but the Dominican author adds that this is not likely, as Fra Giovanni Angelico was at that time in Florence, where the restoration of San Marco was begun, and also the building of the new convent which he adorned with so many marvellous frescoes.

This would actually signify little. As the picture which is said to have been painted for the church of Sant' Andrea at Brescia was naturally done at Fiesole, this one for Perugia might well have been executed at Florence. But though it recalls the most characteristic works of the artist and, for liveliness of colour and accurate study of form, may be considered one of his most remarkable works, we have no hesitation in ascribing it to his first artistic period. In both these altar-pieces the grouping of the figures is still faithful to Giottesque tradition; it was only later, i.e. when Fra Angelico had felt the artistic influences developing around him, that he placed the figures in one picture on different levels, to make a circle round the Mother of Christ.

The type of the Virgin herself in this Perugian picture is similar to that of the Cortona panel; they both have the eyes wide apart, a short, receding chin, and small mouth; characteristics which are also seen in the angels behind the Virgin's throne in the San Domenico picture at Cortona. From an architectural view the throne has here a much more antique shape than in his later designs, where Renaissance forms predominate. As to the picture at Perugia it has been so restored and arbitrarily put together after the panel was divided, that it affords no serious proof of authenticity.

•

We must therefore conclude that the Perugian one was painted before 1433, for could we possibly admit (as Padre Bottonio wills it) that it was done in 1437, that is only a year before the celebrated painting for the church of San Marco? And seeing that when the Dominicans again obtained possession of their own convent and returned to Fiesole neither Fra Angelico nor his brother Fra Benedetto were among them, we may reasonably suppose that Angelico was then at Perugia, painting the altar-piece for the Guidalotti Chapel; and that he only returned to Florence when he had finished that work, which we may date later than the panel still to be admired at Cortona.

These are the only works known to have been painted by him while he and his brethren had left their beloved Fiesole hills to seek peace and tranquillity in Umbria, – the only records of that period of voluntary exile.

II

FRA ANGELICO AT FIESOLE

[1418-1436]

Whilst Fra Angelico was putting the legends of the Virgin and St. Dominic into colour in Umbria, Giovanni Dominici together with Leonardo Dati, master-general of the Order, was negotiating with the Bishop of Fiesole and Pope Gregory XII. to again obtain possession of the convent founded by Dominici. It was only in 1418 that the Fiesolan bishop acceded to their request, on condition that the Dominicans would make him a present of some sacred vestments to the value of a hundred ducats. This sum, writes Marchese, was taken from the legacy left to the convent by the father of St. Antonino, who died about that time. A rich merchant having died in Florence in the same year, leaving the monks of Fiesole six thousand florins, it was besides decided to enlarge the building. The legal act of free and absolute concession being signed, the father-general at once sent for four of the monks from Cortona, among whom, as we have said, were neither Fra Angelico nor Fra Benedetto. This does not imply that all the others who had left in 1409, might not have returned later, and probably Fra Angelico among them.[*16]

It was in this convent from which on the side towards the ridge of the Fiesole hill, he looked on the olives spreading their silvery branches against the blue sky, that Fra Angelico, absorbed in work and prayer, passed the greater part of his life. It is impossible to determine at which of the many works that now adorn the Florentine and foreign galleries, he worked during his stay in Fiesole, where he remained till 1436; certainly he painted the panel pictures for his church, the Tabernacle of the Linen Weavers, and frescoes in some parts of the convent. That convent so dear to him must have awakened in his soul many bitter and sweet memories – whether he thought of the days when he and his brother Benedetto first took their vows, or of the successive vicissitudes when he and the brethren were forced to abandon it.

Vasari asserts that "he painted an Easter candle in several small scenes, for Giovanni Masi, a monk of the convent of Santa Maria Novella; and also some reliquaries which on solemn feast days were placed on the altar," and are preserved to this day in the convent of San Marco. They represent the "Coronation of the Virgin," the "Madonna della Stella" and the "Adoration of the Magi." The Coronation has been too much damaged by useless retouching to be able fully to judge of its merits. It is for this cause perhaps that some people have ventured to doubt its authenticity: "one perceives," writes Cartier, "his religious conception, and desire to follow his model, but the whole composition lacks order and space, the figures are heavy, attitudes embarrassed, proportions short, outlines coarse and the whole painting is strained."[*17]

Now this is not absolutely exact. Naturally if we compare this little reliquary with the great "Coronation" at the Louvre, we find the composition more compressed, but it is not confused. True, the types of the Virgin and Redeemer have not that grand simplicity which with sincere enthusiasm we admire in his later panels of the same subject. But possibly we have here the artist's first conception, an idea which he successively developed and perfected till he reached the highest grade of beauty, first in the picture at the Louvre, then in the truly celestial one of the Florentine Gallery.

In the little painting of the Madonna della Stella (of the Star) we have qualities of grace and nobility all Fra Angelico's own. The six adoring angels on the slope of the frame, and the two seated at the base playing musical instruments, not only fully reveal his ability, but might be classed with those of the Linen Weaver's Tabernacle as among the most beautiful and ethereal he ever painted.

The third reliquary which is divided into two parts represents the "Adoration of the Magi," below, and the "Annunciation" above. The Virgin has a book on her lap, her arms crossed on the breast, and head extended towards the celestial messenger who kneels before her; but both figures, though showing Fra Angelico's characteristic sentiment, have exaggerated proportions; the neck is inordinately long, the colouring enamelled, and so brilliant as to give the picture the character of a fine and elegantly illuminated missal. In the "Adoration" the Virgin displays the same defects of proportion, but among the figures of the three Kings and the personages accompanying them, are some of exceptional elegance and exquisite beauty. On the whole the scene may be classed among the finest and most graceful of the works which Fra Angelico has left to us.

There is a kind of reliquary in the Vatican Gallery, which represents the Virgin seated, with the Child on her left arm. Her raised right hand holds the rose, and at her feet kneel St. Dominic and St. Catherine. Cavalcaselle supposes this to have been the fourth of the reliquaries once in Santa Maria Novella, but it more probably belongs to that small painting reproduced by Prof. Helbig,[*18] in the *Revue de l'Art Chrétien*, in which Angelico has represented the death and assumption of the Virgin.

The under part of the picture, representing the death of the Virgin, recalls, in the general grouping of figures, the same subject now in the Uffizi Gallery; but in this one, four Apostles are depicted in the act of raising the bier, while the others surround the Christ, who holds in His arms the soul of His Mother in the form of a babe. In the upper part we see the Virgin with upraised arms, being received by the Saviour who extends His hands as if in welcome. The type of the Virgin recalls that of the small panel representing the "Adoration" and "Annunciation." The Christ is, in the foreshortening and character of the face, a repetition of that on the reliquary of the "Madonna della Stella." The figure of the Virgin is incorporeal and insignificant; but the angels who in varied attitudes dance around the throne playing divers instruments, are charming and graceful.

•

In the ancient refectory of the Fiesolan convent Fra Angelico painted a life-size Christ Crucified, with St. Dominic kneeling below clinging passionately to the Cross. At the sides stand the Virgin and St. John the Evangelist; there is also a figure of the saintly founder, but it was either added later, or else has been badly restored and cannot be taken as Fra Angelico's work. The picture has been removed from the wall, and is now in the Museum of the Louvre; it is damaged in several parts; the delicacy of colouring is lost, the background spoiled, and only the figures of the Saviour, the Virgin, and the head of St. John remain in tolerable condition.

The other fresco in the old chapter-house (this also has been removed from the wall, and is now in the Hermitage at St. Petersburg), represents the Virgin seated, with the Child on her knee, between St. Dominic and St. Thomas Aquinas; all these figures show signs of incompetent restoration, the outlines and drapery having been repainted. Less spoiled perhaps by retouching, but yet in a deplorable condition, is the other painting, a Crucifixion, still existing in the Sacristy of the Convent. The Redeemer with extended arms, has His head drooping straight on the breast, and the legs are stiffened and curve to the right. A crown of thorns encircles the head, which is surrounded by a great aureole; but the head is small; and the face, with its insignificant features, lacks the intense expression which Fra Angelico usually succeeds in putting into similar subjects.

·

He also painted the altar-piece for the great altar in San Domenico at Fiesole, "which," writes Vasari,

> perhaps because it appeared to be deteriorating, has been retouched and injured by other masters. But the predella and ciborium of the Sacrament are better preserved; and you may see infinite little figures which are lovely in their celestial glory, and appear indeed to come from Paradise, nor can those who draw near ever look at them sufficiently."[*19]

The picture is now removed into the choir. In the centre the Virgin with her Son, is seated on the throne; six angels stand around her in act of adoration, and two kneel in front with vases in their hands. At the sides St. Thomas and St. Peter are placed on the left; St. Dominic and St. Peter Martyr on the right. The retouching of which Vasari speaks, was done by Lorenzo di Credi in 1501, when the picture was reduced to its present form. We learn this from a record in the MS. chronicle of the Convent of Fiesole, which is quoted by Padre Marchese in his "Memorie."[*20] But the panel has suffered other and worse things than this. Other figures taken from an older frame have been substituted for those in the pilasters. Some coarse copies have been put in the place of the three "stories" of the predella, and the original one was sold, together with the ciborium.[*21]

The predella, now in the National Gallery of London, is divided into five compartments. In the centre is Christ robed in white, His right hand raised in benediction, and a standard held in His left; at the sides are a crowd of angels – some blowing trumpets, others playing instruments, others again in attitudes of profound veneration – all have robes of pure and brilliant hues with azure wings lightly sprinkled with gold. The side scenes have multitudes of saints, either standing or kneeling in adoration: on the left are patriarchs, bishops, monks and martyrs, each with his own emblem; on the right, a crowd of kneeling feminine saints among whom we can recognise St. Agnes, St. Catherine and St. Helen, and behind them a line of male saints, amongst them St. Cyprian, St. Clement, St. Thomas, St. Erasmus, and others whose names are written on their mitres. Still higher King David, St. John Baptist and the prophets Jeremiah, Zaccariah and Habakkuk. The faces are painted with great delicacy and accuracy, and although they show some variety of lineament, the expression is rather mannered. The outlines of the feminine saints are full of grace and those of the other sex do not lack great dignity. Although the work is of minor proportion, it shows a noteworthy progress when compared with the conceptions of Orcagna.

The greater part of the draperies are rendered with most refined colouring, so delicately toned and judiciously contrasted, that no part of the painting appears either crude, or of exaggerated richness; while the gold used in every part of the background contributes to give great harmony to the whole. In the pictures placed at the end of the predella, the Dominicans are depicted in their white robes and black mantles.

This delightful work, which roused the admiration of Vasari, contains not less than 266 figures and may justly be considered as one of the gems of the collection. Executed with all the delicacy of an illumination, it sparkles with bright but harmonious colours, while the spirit of devotion which penetrates the whole is entirely characteristic of the painter.[*22]

•

Fra Angelico reached greater perfection in the picture of the "Annunciation" of which Vasari says: "In a chapel of the same church is a picture from the same hand, representing Our Lady receiving the Annunciation from the angel Gabriel, with a countenance which is seen in profile, so devout, so delicate, and so perfectly executed, that the beholder can scarcely believe it to be by the hand of man, but would rather suppose it to have been delineated in Paradise. In the landscape forming the background are seen Adam and Eve, whose fall made it needful that the Virgin should give birth to the Redeemer."[*23]

This picture (purchased in 1611 by Duke Mario Farnese) is now in the Museum at Madrid. The Virgin is seated on the right under a graceful portico sustained by small columns. Her head inclines a little towards the Angel, in the same attitude as in the Cortona altar-piece and the fresco at San Marco. She holds the book on her knees, and crosses her hands on her breast; while the golden winged Angel, in its rose coloured robe, with an arm curved in similar attitude of reverence, sheds light around, as in the painting at Cortona. High up in the left corner the hand of the Eternal Father sends down a ray of light, in the midst of which the Holy Spirit is symbolized. In the background, as in the Cortona picture, Adam and Eve are being expelled from Paradise.

In the predella are some beautiful "stories" representing the "Marriage of the Virgin," the "Salutation," the "Adoration of the Magi," the "Circumcision of Christ" and the "Death of the Virgin."[*24]

"But superior to all the other works of Fra Giovanni, and one in which he surpassed himself, is a picture in the same church (i.e. San Domenico at Fiesole), near the door on the left hand of the entrance: in this work, he proves the high quality of his powers as well as the profound intelligence he possessed of the art which he practised. The subject is the Coronation of the Virgin by Jesus Christ: the principal figures are surrounded by a choir of angels, among whom are vast numbers of saints and holy personages, male and female. These figures are so numerous, so well executed, in attitudes so varied, and the expressions of the heads so richly diversified, that one feels infinite pleasure and delight in regarding them. Nay, one is convinced that those blessed spirits can look no otherwise in heaven itself, or to speak under correction, could not, if they had forms, appear otherwise; for all the saints, male and female, assembled here, have not only life and expression, most delicately and truly rendered, but the colouring also of the whole work would seem to have been given by the hand of a saint, or of an angel like themselves. It is not without sufficient reason therefore, that this excellent ecclesiastic is always called Frate Giovanni Angelico. The stories from the life of Our Lady and of St. Dominic which adorn the predella, moreover, are in the same divine style; and I, for myself, can affirm with truth, that I never see this work but it appears something new, nor can I ever satisfy myself with the sight of it, or have enough of beholding it."[*25]

The painting is now in the Louvre at Paris, having been taken from Fiesole during the French invasion of 1812.

Under a rich canopy with inlaid columns and brocade hangings the Redeemer seated on the throne, places the crown on the head of his Mother, who kneels before him, with hands crossed on her bosom. Around them angels are making the air resound with the voice of song, and the music of many instruments. Saints, male and female circle round, some standing, others kneeling, their fixed eyes and ecstatic features denoting their joy in such divine splendour. Among the saints are the great personages of the religious orders, together with bishops and emperors. On the right, among the kneeling female saints are seen St. Agnes tenderly pressing the lamb to her breast, St. Catherine holding her wheel of torture and a palm, St. Ursula clasps the arrow which united her in death to her divine Spouse, St. Cecilia's pretty head is garlanded with flowers, while St. Mary Magdalene turns her back showing the rich locks of hair flowing over her shoulder as she holds the vase of ointment in her left hand. On the opposite side are St. Dominic with the lily and open book, St. Augustine, St. Benedict, St. Anthony and St. Francis. On a higher level St. Louis, with his crown of *fiordalise*, talks with St. Thomas; while St. Nicholas supports himself with both hands on his pastoral staff.

"It is a clever composition, wonderfully balanced, and the solemnity of style does not at all exclude exuberance of life or infinite variety of ideas.
"The bodies are almost diaphanous, the heads ethereal, the atmosphere and light have a touch of the supernatural. Up to this point the subject is subdued, but the colours lively and pure – among which blue and carmine predominate – gleam with particular splendour."[*26]

The predella contains in some small compositions the chief episodes in the life of St. Dominic, excepting the central compartment where Christ is drawn, issuing from the sepulchre between the Virgin and St. John. The compositions are all executed with that love and delicacy which are the glory of the artist, but even these little stories, like the larger panel, have been more or less injured by repeated restorations.

A similar subject now in the Uffizi Gallery at Florence and which Fra Angelico painted for the church of Santa Maria Novella, is still more aerial and celestial, a perfect masterpiece of sentiment and mystic expression.

Here also Fra Angelico clings to that traditional characteristic, peculiarly his own – the art of sacred vision, but with what new life he animates it, and what poetical witchery he throws into this creation of his ascetic fantasy!

His predecessors reproduced with slight varieties the model of Giotto, and the great Florentine painter himself has given us the scene in its most simple reality. High in the central part of Giotto's "Coronation" Christ places the crown on the Virgin, who with hands crossed, bows her head to receive the homage of her Son. But on her face there is no expression of ecstatic joy, modest, indeed "humble in the midst of glory", she droops her eyes, almost as if she dared not rest them on the Saviour. Angels and saints, symmetrically disposed at the sides, fill the whole background of the picture, with heads either raised in admiration or bowed in respect, but in attitudes so similar, that they give a sense of monotony. Then come the saints, some kneeling at the foot of the throne, and others in the side wings of the triptych, reverently bowing to the Mother of God.

Fra Angelico repeats the principal motive, but develops it according to his high ideal, his intense faith, and mystic sentiment. He gives to the Virgin an expression of infinite sweetness; to the angels a truly celestial charm, to the saints a serene expression of beatitude, and to the whole scene the azure divine character of a vision of Paradise.

High in the centre the Redeemer extends his right hand to add a brilliant gem to the crown of the Virgin, who sits near him, with hands crossed in loving reverence. A luminous golden ray from this group engraved on the panel, forms gleaming and resplendent waves in the background of the picture, from which groups of angels stand out, playing all sorts of music, or dancing with hand clasped in hand. Two are prostrated in profound admiration at the base, and shed clouds of incense from their thuribles, while two others draw melody from heavenly harps.

In the lower part of the picture are many saints, who by their charmed faces and feeling of ineffable joy, show how delighted they are with the vision and the heavenly music.

> "The greatest eloquence," writes Marchese, "would fail to express the impression which this painting produces. The heart has a language which does not always speak in words, and we can never contemplate this picture without feeling in love with heaven."[*27]
>
> •

Among the works which were undoubtedly done by Fra Angelico during his stay at Fiesole, may be ascribed several different representations of the Last Judgment. He derived the inspiration of the subject directly from Orcagna's fresco in Santa Maria Novella, only Fra Angelico has created a paradise too exclusively modelled on the monastic life. "His ideal," writes Reymond, "is a young neophyte entirely absorbed in prayer – a contemplative being who has renounced earthly life, abdicating his qualities as a man to dream of nothing but the future life. Orcagna, on the contrary, dreams of an ideal in which human life triumphs in all its fulness, and one might say that the beings which people his Paradise are but glorified bodies."[*28]

Fra Giovanni painted Hell and Paradise with small figures for the Camaldolese monks of Santa Maria degli Angeli. This is the picture now in the Ancient and Modern Gallery at Florence, of which Vasari writes, "he proved the rectitude of his judgment in this work, having made the countenances of the blessed beautiful and full of a celestial gladness; but the condemned, those destined to the pains of hell, he has depicted in various attitudes of sorrow, and bearing the impress and consciousness of their misdeeds and wretchedness on their faces: the blessed are seen to enter the gate of paradise in triumphal dance, the condemned are dragged away to eternal punishment in hell by the hands of demons."[*29]

The representation is faithful to artistic tradition. In the highest part the Saviour calls the elect to Him with His right hand, while with His left He motions away the reprobate: around Him are eight winged cherubim, with whom kneeling angels below join to form a circle. Some are adoring or praying, others hold scrolls in their hands. On the right sits the Virgin in white robes, with hands crossed on her breast and head gently bent: on the left St. John Baptist with hands clasped in prayer. At the sides Patriarchs, Apostles and Prophets, and at the extremities St. Dominic and St. Francis. An angel holds the cross at the feet of Christ, and two others flying, blow their trumpets towards the dead, who rise from the open sepulchres below.

In the base at the left, demons drag the damned ones to Hell; on the right the elect cast glances of love and faith on the Saviour, and in joyous fraternity enjoy the heavenly guerdon. The Elysian Fields of the blessed are truly celestial, gleaming with gold, irrigated by limpid streams, glorious with beautiful flowerets that bloom amid the verdure, the exuberance of nature harmonizing marvelously with the joy of the elect.

> Thousands of angels, in resplendence each
> Distinct and quaint adornment. At their glee
> And carol smiled the Lovely One of heaven
> That joy was in the eyes of all the blest.[*30]

Not unworthy of the divine poet is Angelico's heavenly composition in which as in the Dantesque Paradise is shed

> Light intellectual replete with love,
> Love of true happiness, replete with joy,

Joy, that transcends all sweetness of delight.[*31]

Together with these verses of Dante, Fra Angelico, while endeavouring to depict the dance of the blessed, may well have called to mind these verses of a sacred laud, which is said to be by Iacopone da Todi and (whether his or not) describes in popular language the celestial *caròla*[*32] of the saints:

> Una rota si fa in cielo
> De tutti i Santi in quel zardino,
> Là ove sta l'amor divino
> Che s'infiamma de l'amore.
>
> In quella rota vano i Santi
> Et li Angioli tutti quanti;
> A quello Sposo van davanti:
> Tutti danzan per amore.
>
> In quella corte è un' alegreza
> D' un amor dismisuranza:
> Tutti vanno ad una danza
> Per amor del Salvatore.
>
> Son vestiti di vergato,
> Bianco, rosso e frammezzato;
> Le ghirlande in mezo el capo:
> Ben mi pareno amatori.
>
> Tutti quanti con ghirlandi,
> Paren giovin' de trent' anni:
> Quella corte se rinfranchi,
> Ogni cosa è piena d'amore.
>
> Le ghirlande son fiorite,
> Più che l'oro son chiarite:
> Ornate son di margarite,
> Divisate di colore, ecc.[*33]

Above from the heavenly Jerusalem stream rays of golden light, and two angels who are passing into the portal, are aerial and luminous, as bright and splendid spirits.

•

Less original is the representation of Hell, which is copied straight from the fresco in the Pisan Camposanto. Not only the same division of *bolge* (hell-pits), but even the repetition of motives in the souls that fill them; the only and notable difference is the figure of Lucifer which instead of being in the centre occupies the base of the picture. At the summit "Eriton cruda, che richiamava l'ombre a' corpi sui," is precisely in the same attitude as in the Pisan Camposanto, a figure holding a banner coiled around by a serpent, and near it is a simoniac with his entrails torn out, the identical figure from the Pisan Hell. The back view of the figure which a demon raises to throw into the jaws of a terrible monster is also copied entire from the same fresco.

The *bolge* and the damned souls which occupy them, are, as we have said, repetitions, but with less intelligence and character than the Pisan fresco. On the left the slothful and lazy are punished; beneath them in two *bolge* are the passionate and the gluttonous souls, and below again the luxurious and avaricious ones. The poverty of conception in this "Inferno" is not even compensated by the usual good qualities of refinement; one could almost believe that the artist found it so repugnant to his character to depict brutality and infernal tortures, that he hurried over this part to get rid of it the sooner. The representation of the damned is cold, their struggles with the demons, which at Pisa and in other places is so full of energy, is given here with exaggerated art and becomes ineffectual; in fact this part of the picture is void of feeling, and confirms our previous remarks on the artistic character of the painter.

Another "Last Judgment" is in the Corsini Gallery at Rome; – a triptych, the side panels of which represent the "Ascension" and the "Descent of the Holy Ghost."

This scene is, however, much more simply designed, but cannot be fairly judged now, on account of the retouching and frequent varnishing which disfigure it.

The Saviour seated on the clouds, rests his left hand on a book which he holds upright on his knees, while the right is raised in malediction against the sinners, with an action which recalls the Christ in the Judgment of the Camposanto at Pisa. On the sides are groups of angels, apostles and saints; and the elect are on the right, the wicked on the left below them. "In the picture of the Corsini Gallery," writes Venturi,

> "the representation was cramped by the narrow limits of the central panel of the triptych. It is evidently a reduced form of preceding compositions, for several angels which terminate the picture above, are here seen only from the waist downwards. The figures of the elect, loving, ecstatic and beautiful, clad in flame-coloured robes, with stars and flowers, as in similar compositions by Fra Angelico, are absolutely sublime, while those of the wicked are almost childish, especially the demons with faces of cats and jackals, with red eyes and mouths, black bodies and clawed feet. How much happier he is in the clear and joyful note of colour in some figures standing before a door on the right! And how much better we recognise his sweet spirit in the features of the blest, with their clear eyes whose pupils are fixed trance-like under lightly drawn eyebrows."[*34]

•

Another panel with a subject analogous to these is in the Berlin Museum, and is considered superior to that in the Florentine Gallery.[*35] Although the figure of the Saviour may be slightly wanting in character, the celestial phalanx is full of grace, especially the blessed ones who cross a flower-strewn field to be led by angels up to paradise; they hold each others hands, and dance and sing delightfully and with graceful action and attitudes raise their heads to join in the glory of *Colui che tutto move e risplende*

Nel ciel che più della sua luce prende.

Another last Judgment forms one of the thirty-five small pictures which adorned the doors of the presses for the silver vessels etc., in the chapel of the SS. Annunziata. It is generally believed that he painted this during his stay at Fiesole; but as we find it dates posterior to this, we shall speak of it later, and must first record that in 1432 Fra Angelico painted an "Annunciation" for the church of Sant' Alessandro at Brescia, said to be the one on an altar to the right on entering the church. So greatly is it transformed by restorations, that no one in looking at it now would dream that it was by our artist, if indeed it ever were his work. It would appear that the restorer had used other models in repainting the Angel and the Virgin.[*36]

On July 11th 1433 the contract was signed between the Consuls of the Arte dei Linaioli (Guild of Linen Weavers) and our artist, for the tabernacle of which they had asked Lorenzo Ghiberti to give a design. The contract says:

> "We engage Fra Guido, called Fra Giovanni of the Order of St. Dominic of Fiesole, to paint for the said Guild, a tabernacle of Our Lady; to be painted within and without with colours, gold, azure and silver, all of the very finest that can be found, with all his art and diligence, and for all this and his fatigue and work, he shall receive one hundred and ninety gold florins, or any less sum as shall appear to his conscience, and in consideration of the figures that are in the design."

This painting is now to be admired in the Uffizi Gallery where it was placed in 1777; it is too universally known to need a minute description. The Virgin enthroned with the Holy Child is surrounded by twelve angels, the most lovely, graceful and celestial that Fra Angelico ever painted. In the interior of the side panels are St. John and St. Mark, in the exterior St. Peter and St. Mark. The latter, as is well known, was the protector of the Linen Guild: "therefore," says Padre Marchese, "they wished that whether the tabernacle were open or closed, he should be always in their sight."

In this work Fra Angelico shows that his style was derived from Giotto and Orcagna, though his figures with their large heads, are treated like miniatures and become insignificant; the result is cold and void, precisely by reason of this over conscientious execution.

The face of the Virgin lacks expression and sentiment, while the angels depicted on the slope of the frame in act of sounding trumpets, psalters, cymbals etc., have such a sweetness of sentiment that they seem literally rained down from heaven.

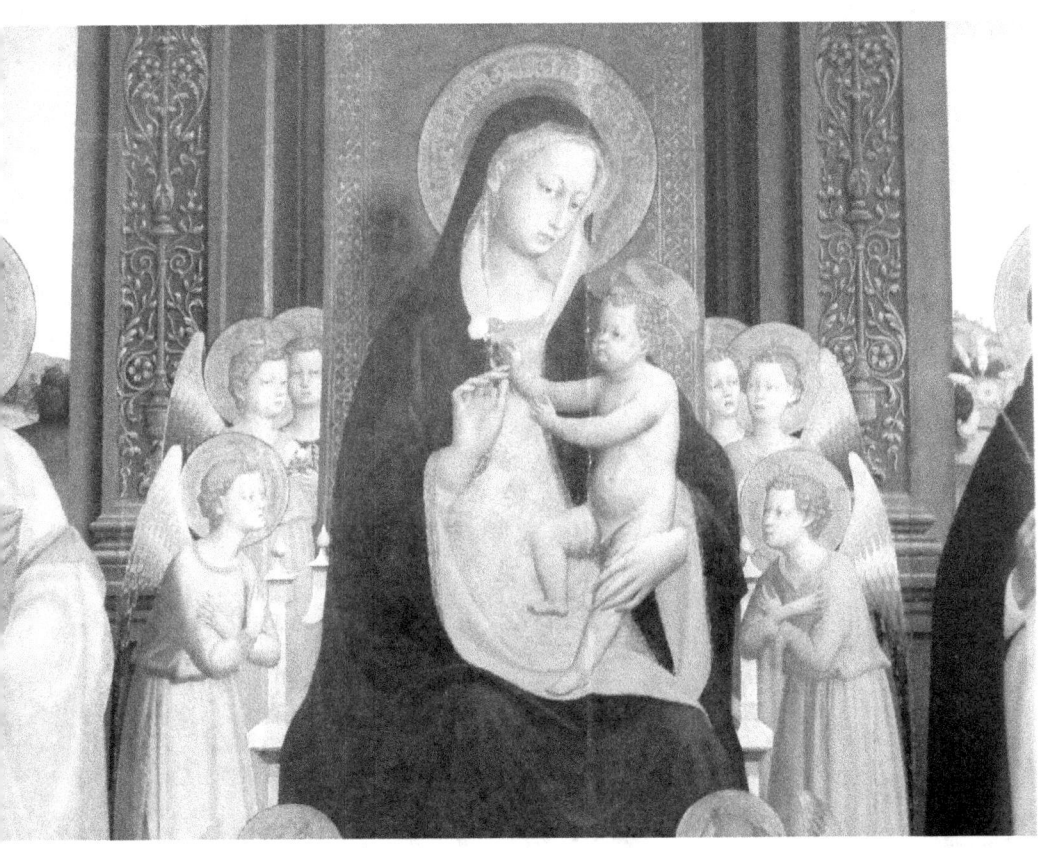

Fra Angelico, Virgin and Child, Fiesole

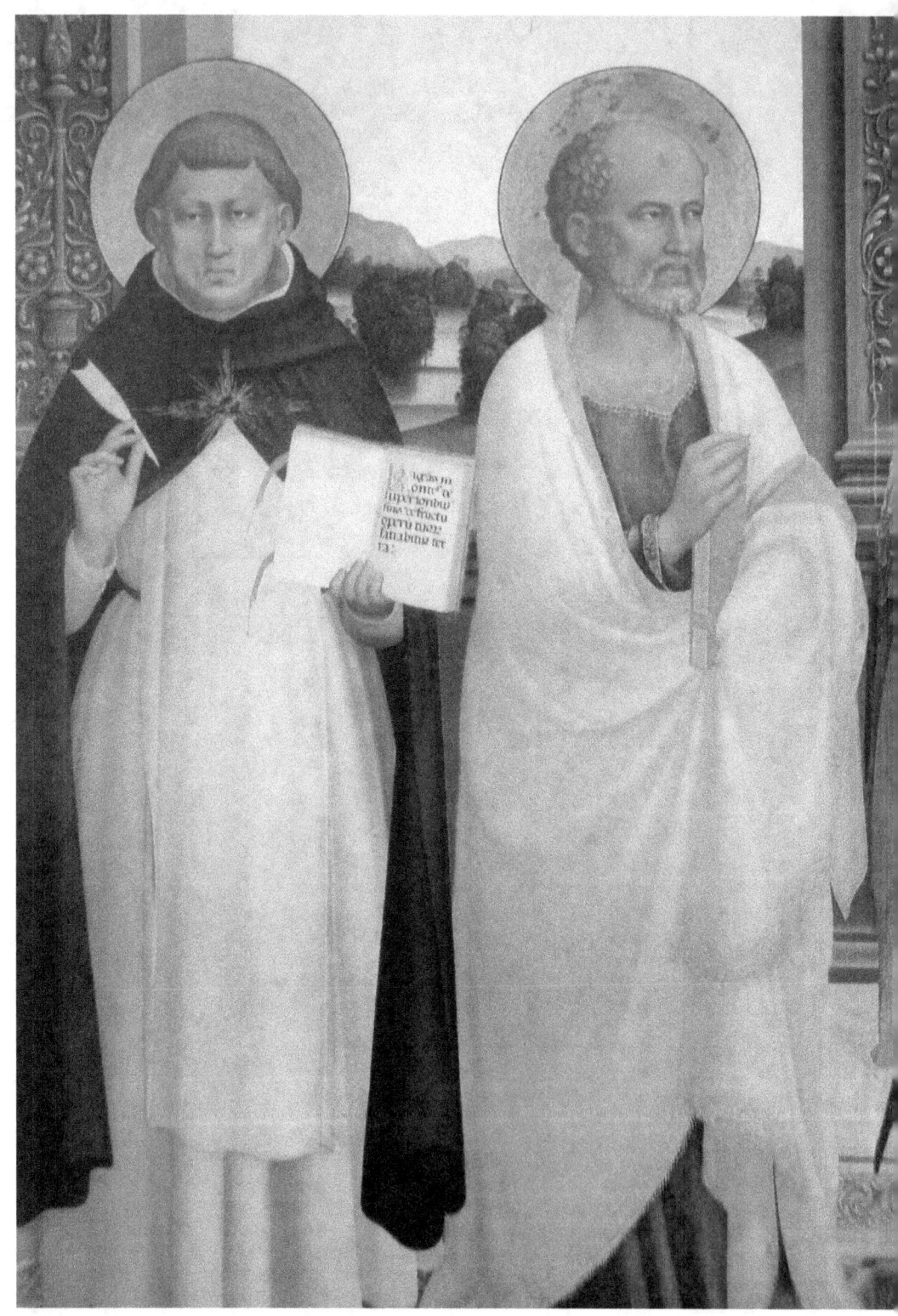

Fra Angelico, Virgin and Child Enthroned, c. 1424-25, detail, Fiesole

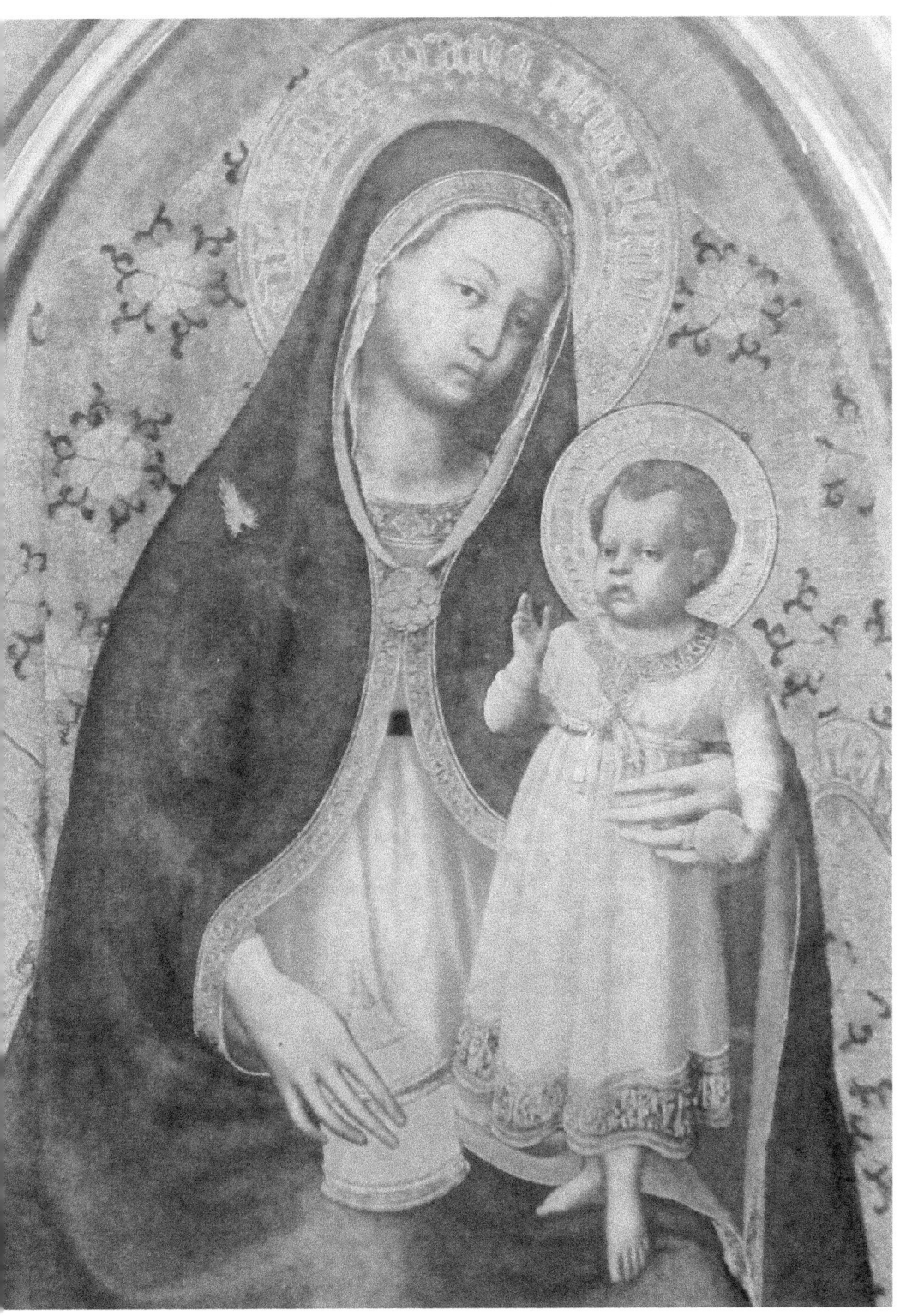

Fra Angelico, San Pier Martire Altarpiece

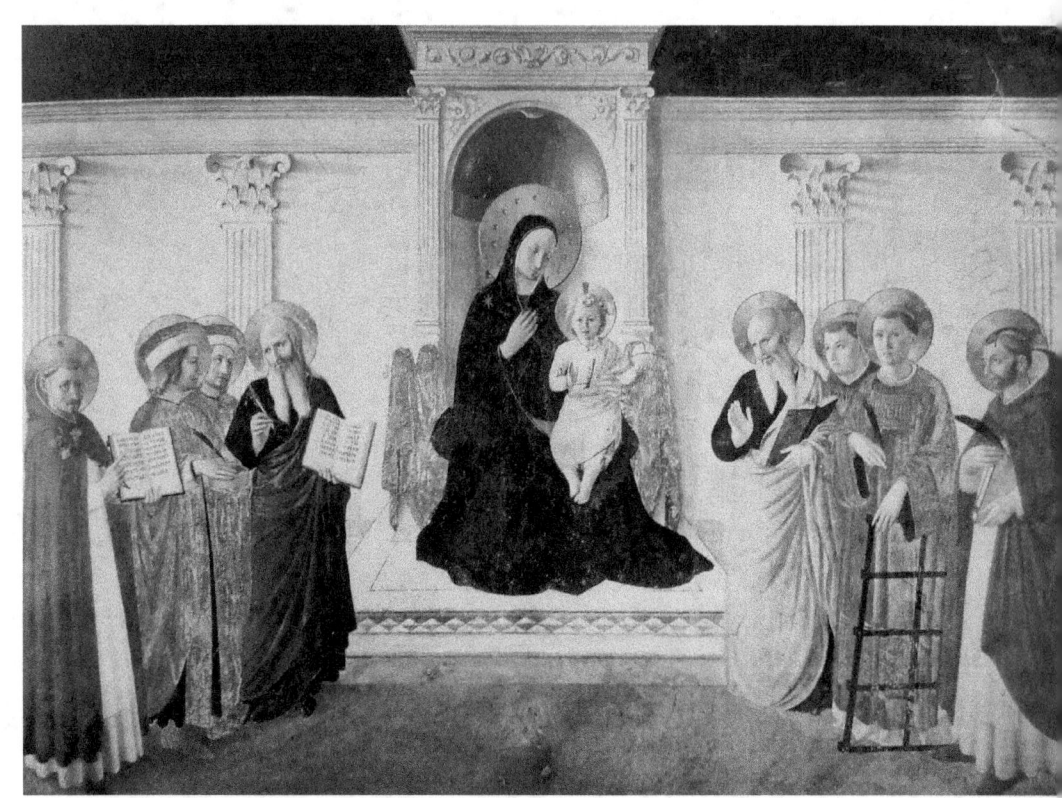

Fra Angelico, Sacra Conversazione, 1440

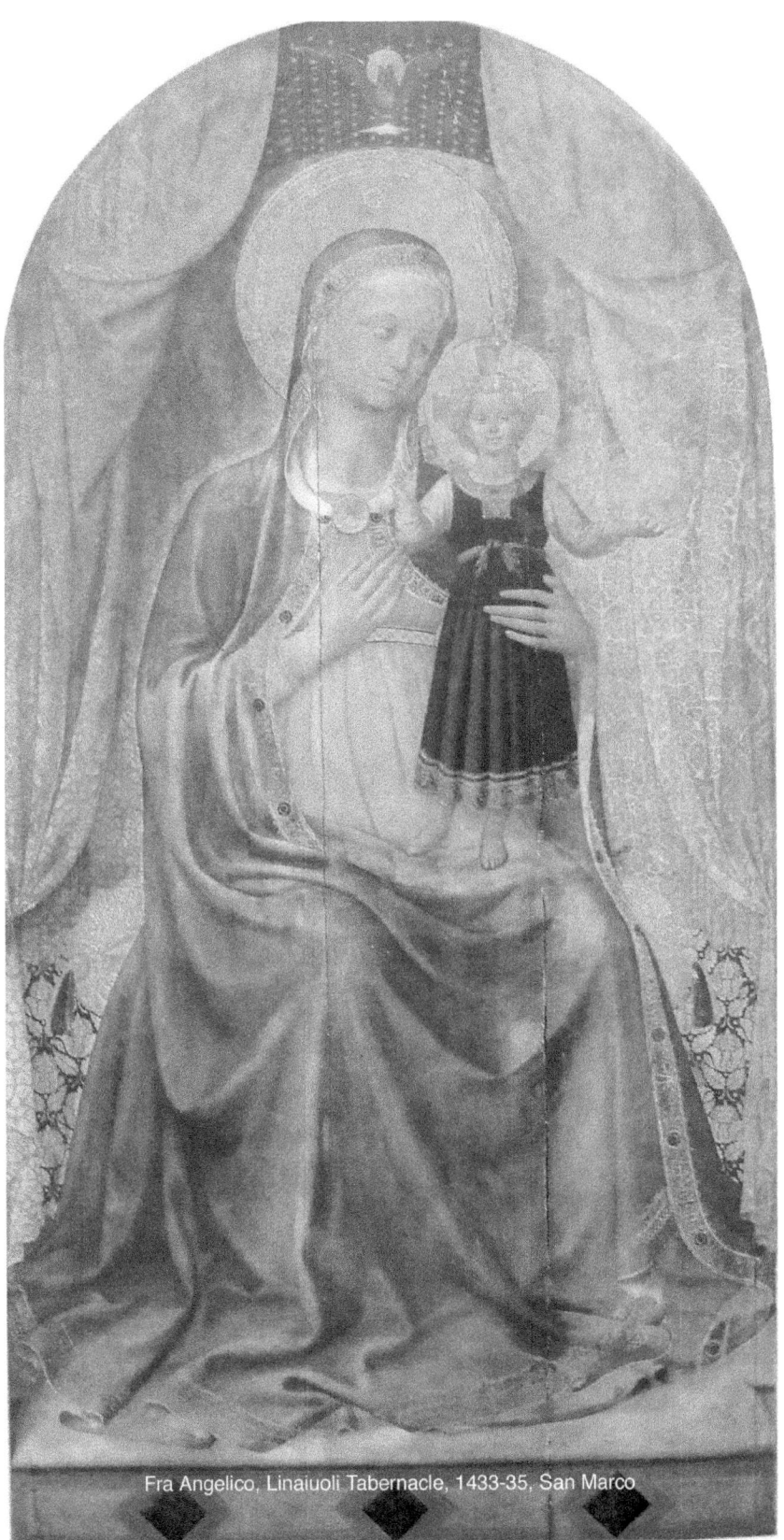

Fra Angelico, Linaiuoli Tabernacle, 1433-35, San Marco

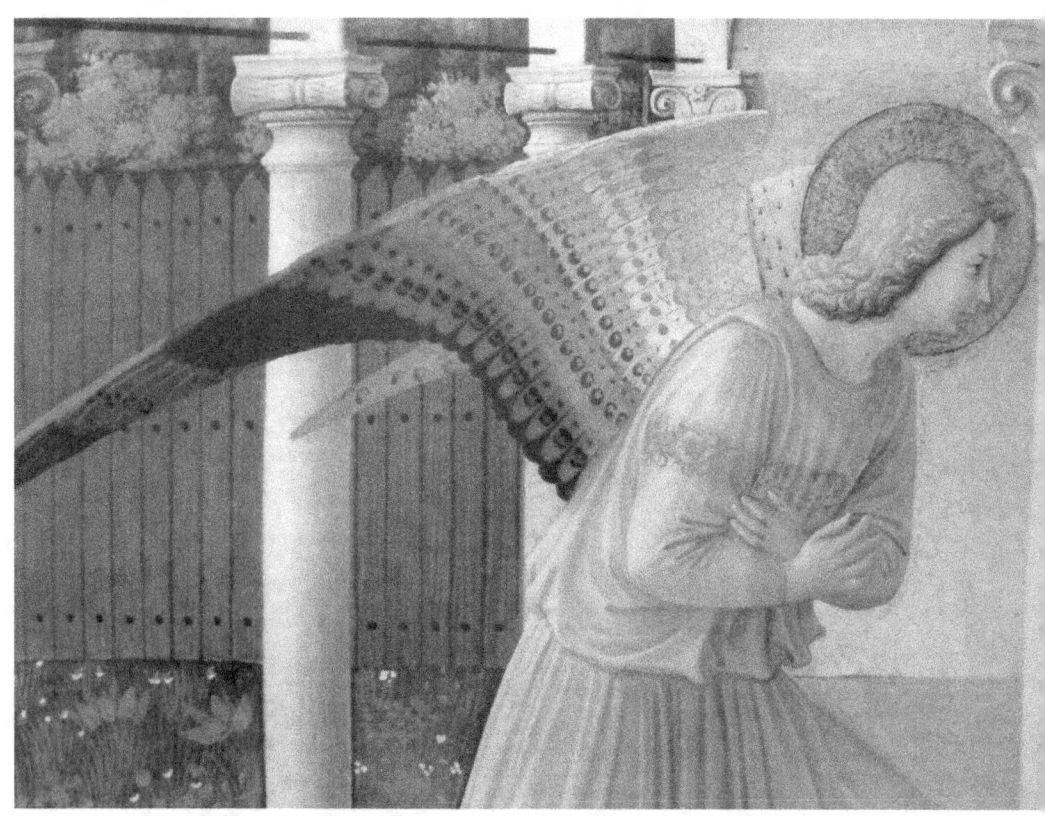

Fra Angelico, Annunciation, c. 1450, detail, upper corridor, San Marco

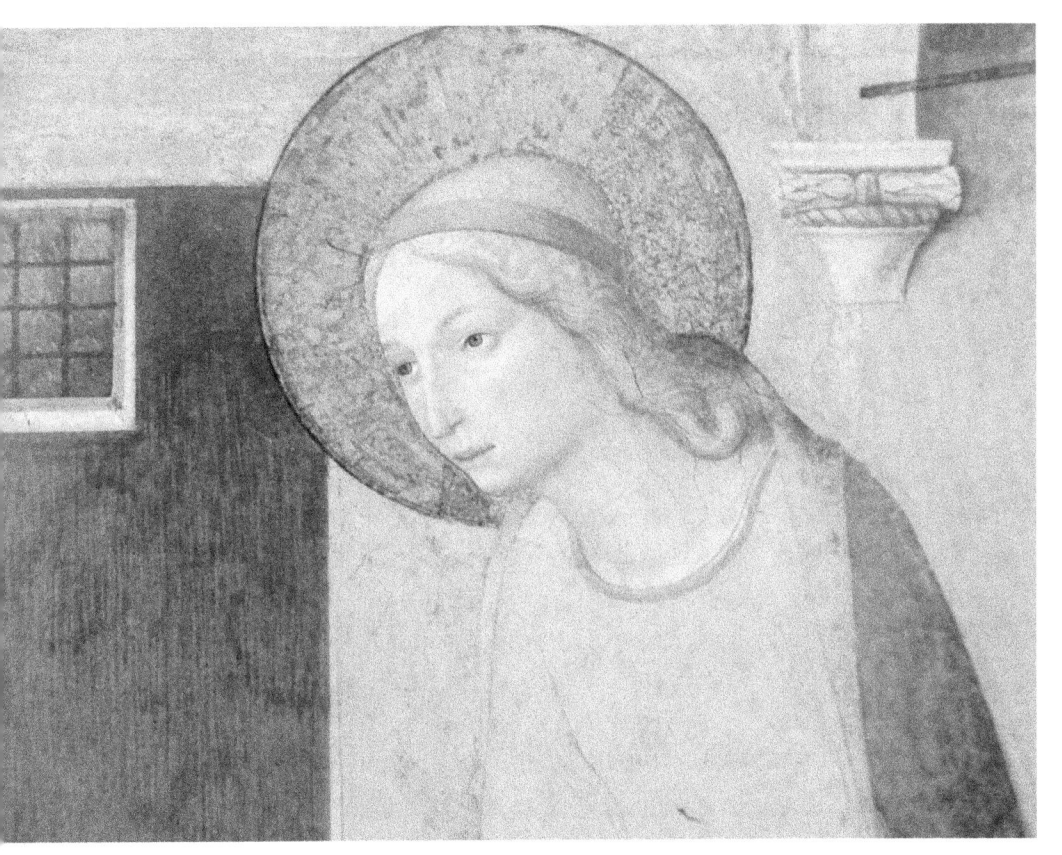

Fra Angelico, Annunciation, detail, San Marco, Florence

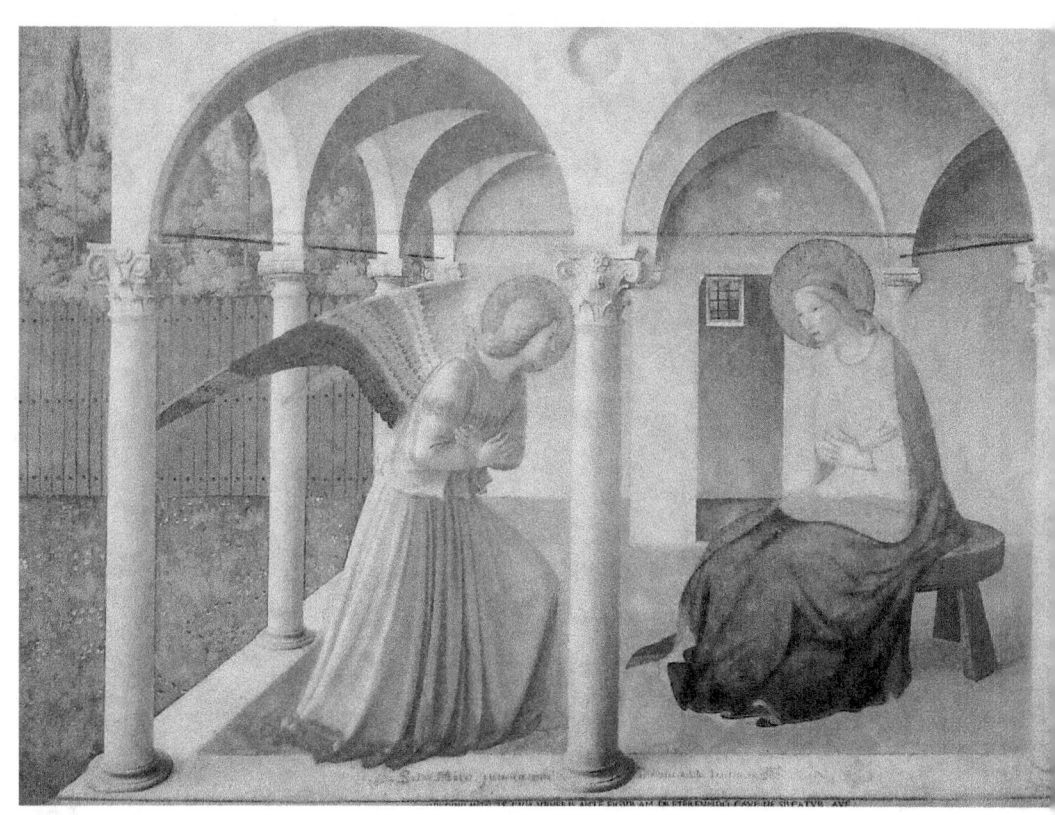

Fra Angelico, The Annunciation, San Marco, Florence

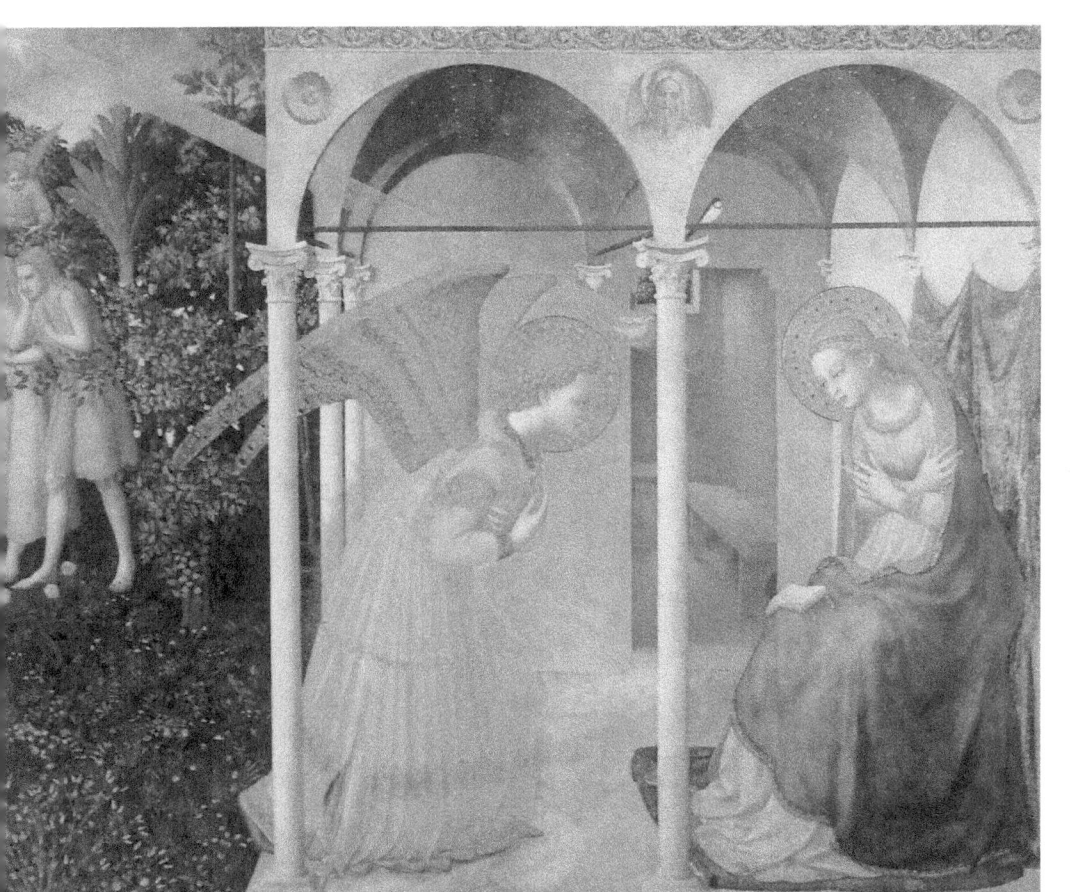

Fra Angelico, Annunciation, Prado, Madrid

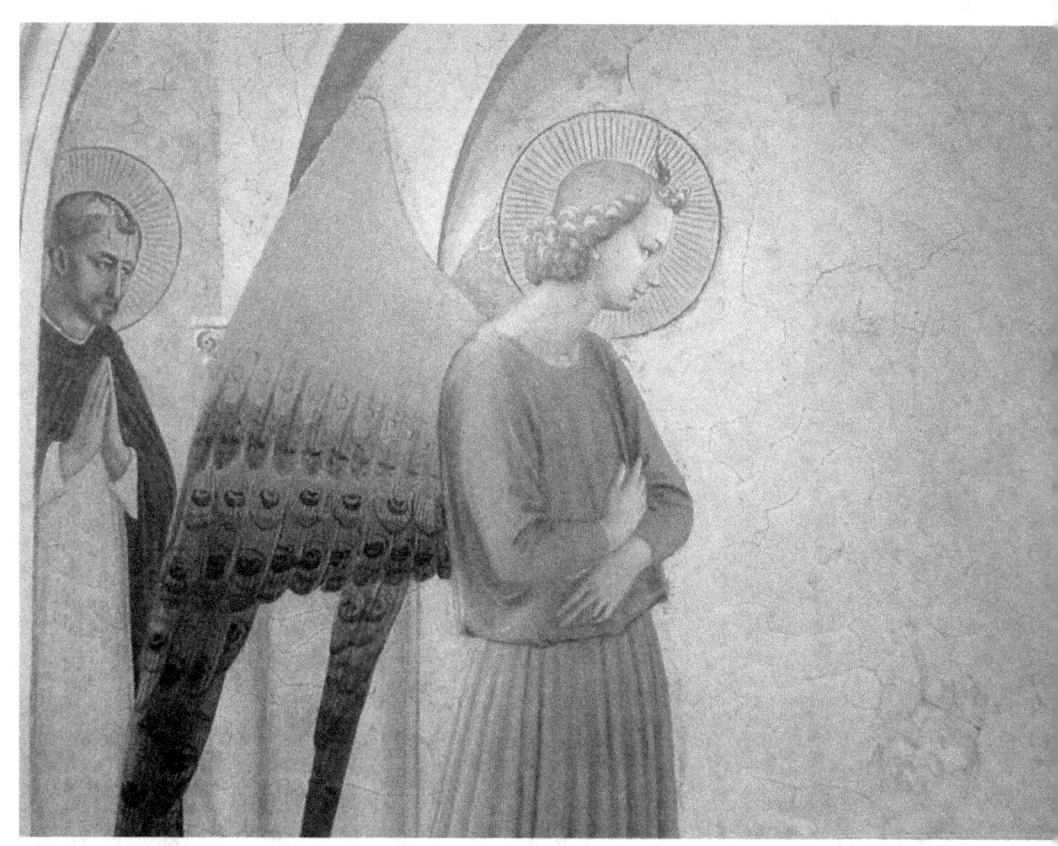

Fra Angelico, Annunciation, cell 3, San Marco

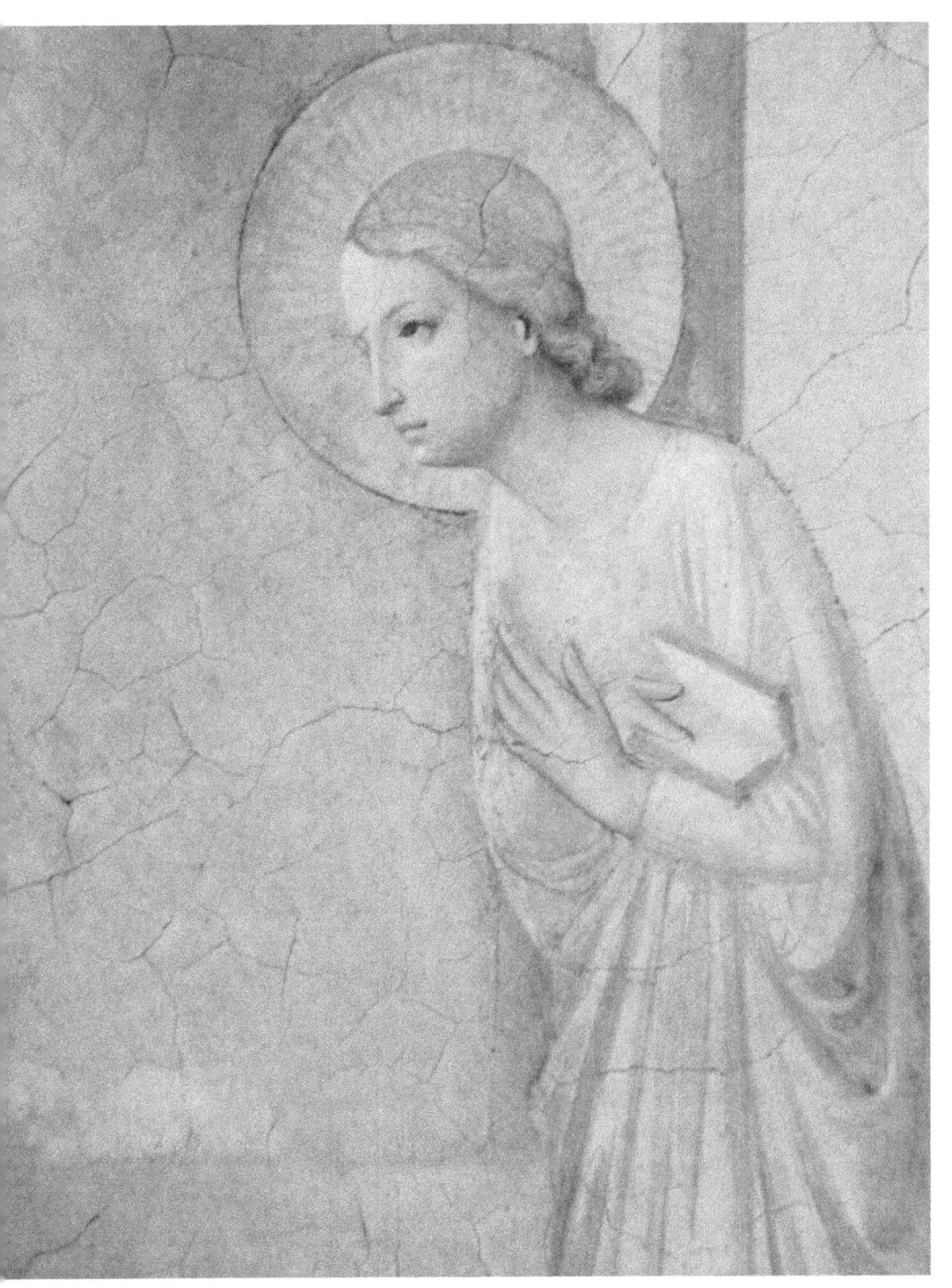

Fra Angelico, Annunciation, cell 3 at San Marco

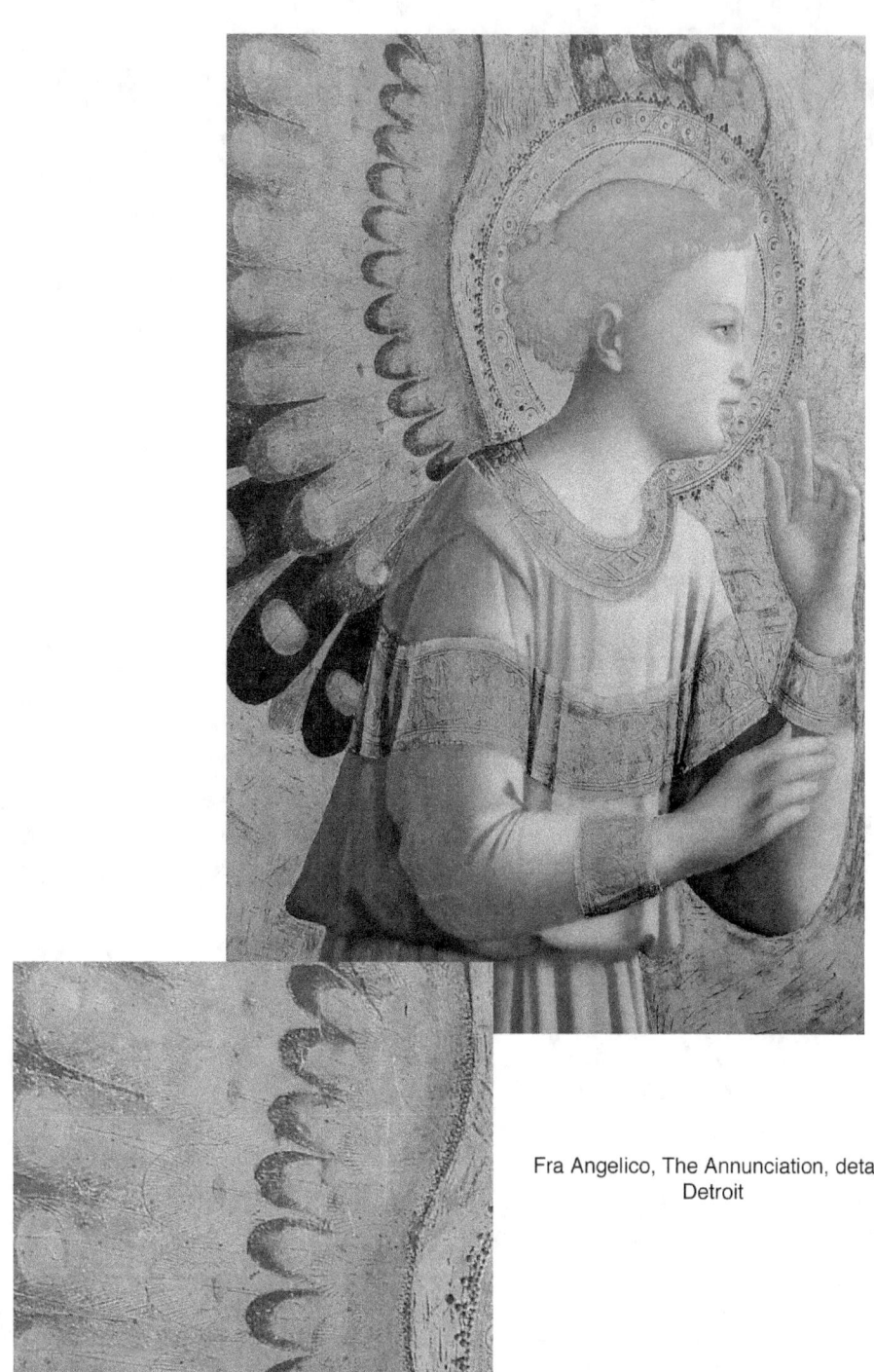

Fra Angelico, The Annunciation, detail, Detroit

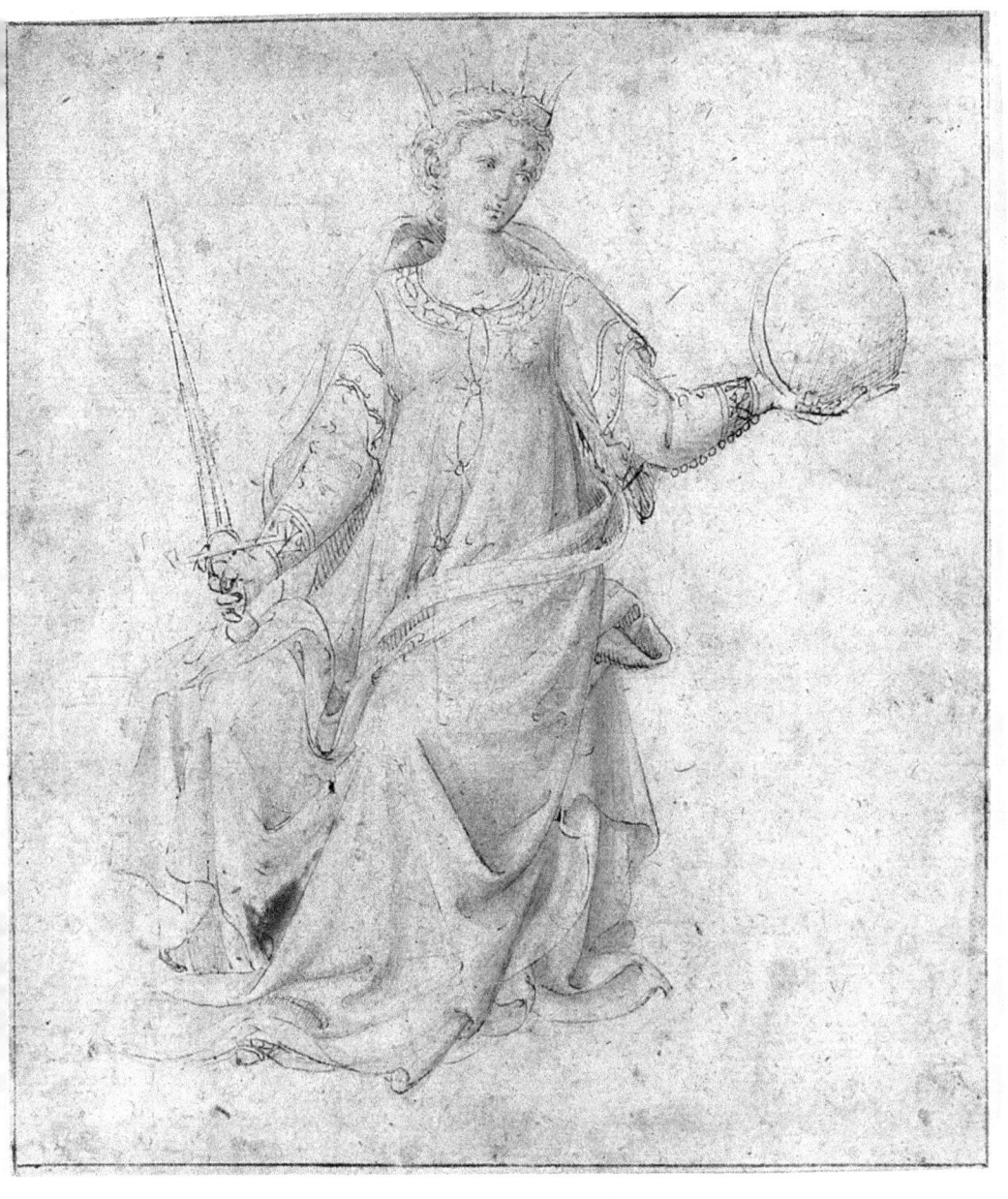

Fra Angelico, Justice, Metropolitan Museum of Art, NYC

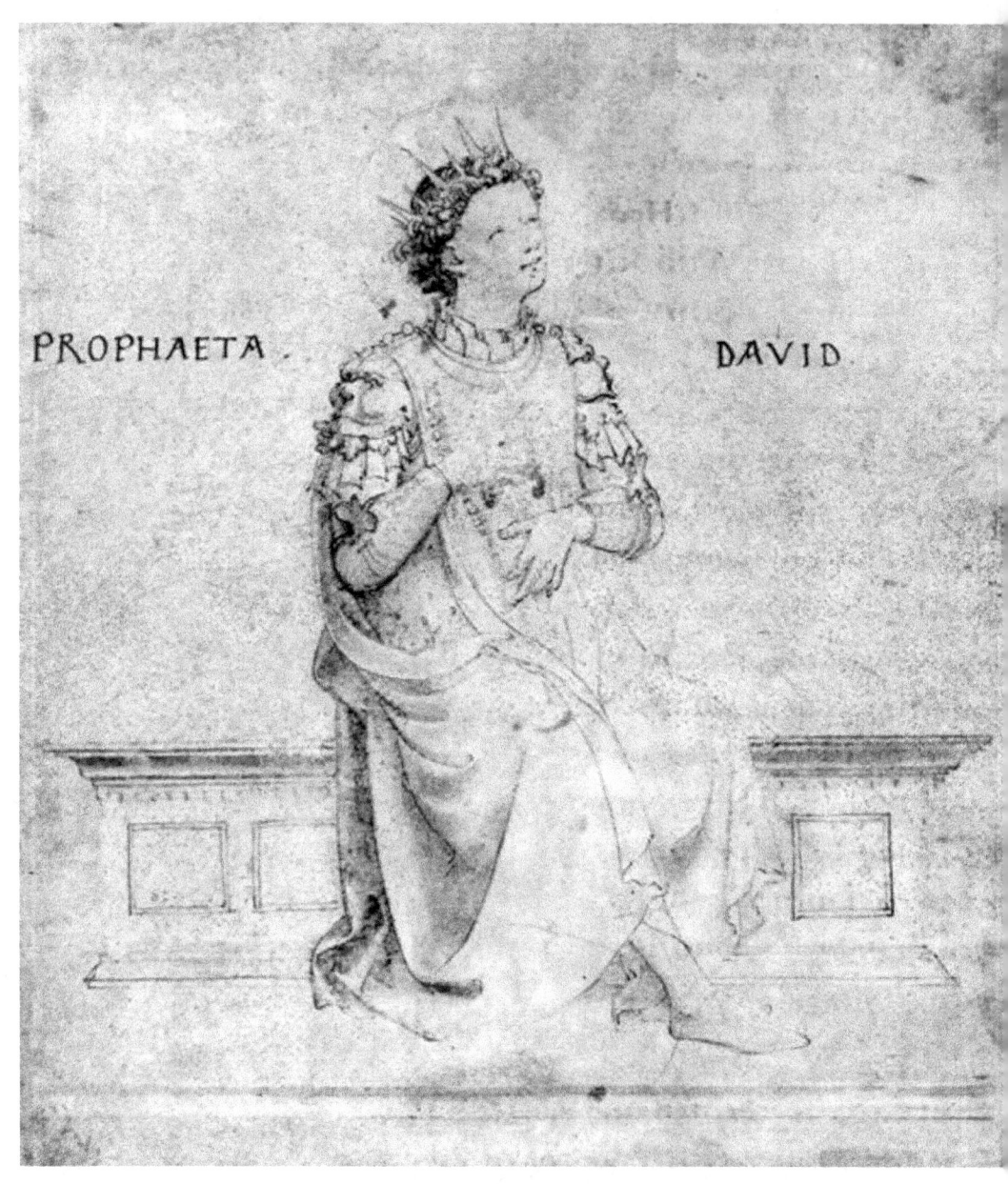

PROPHAETA . DAVID

Fra Angelico, King David, 1430, San Marco

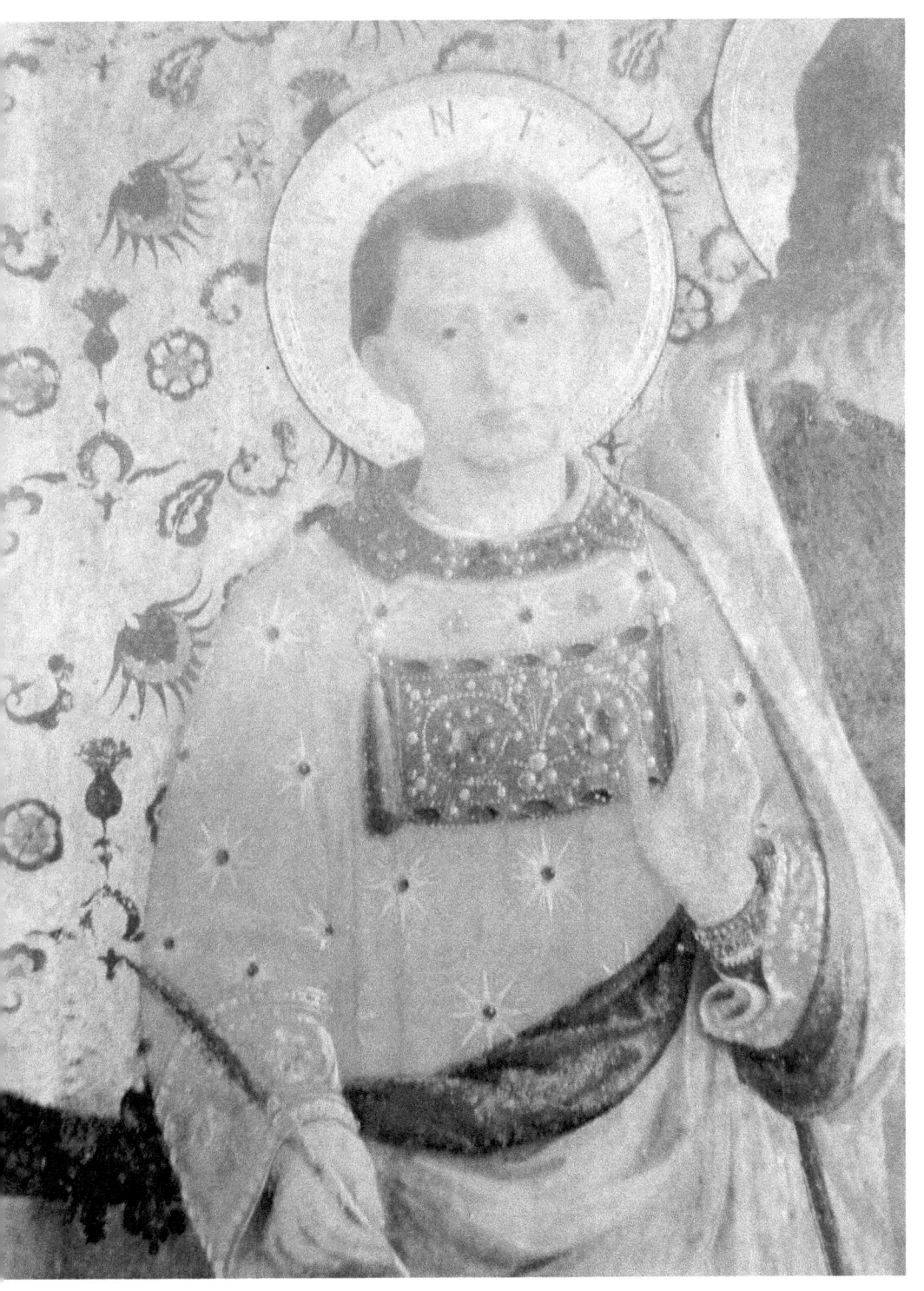

Fra Angelico, San Marco Altarpiece, 1438-40, detail

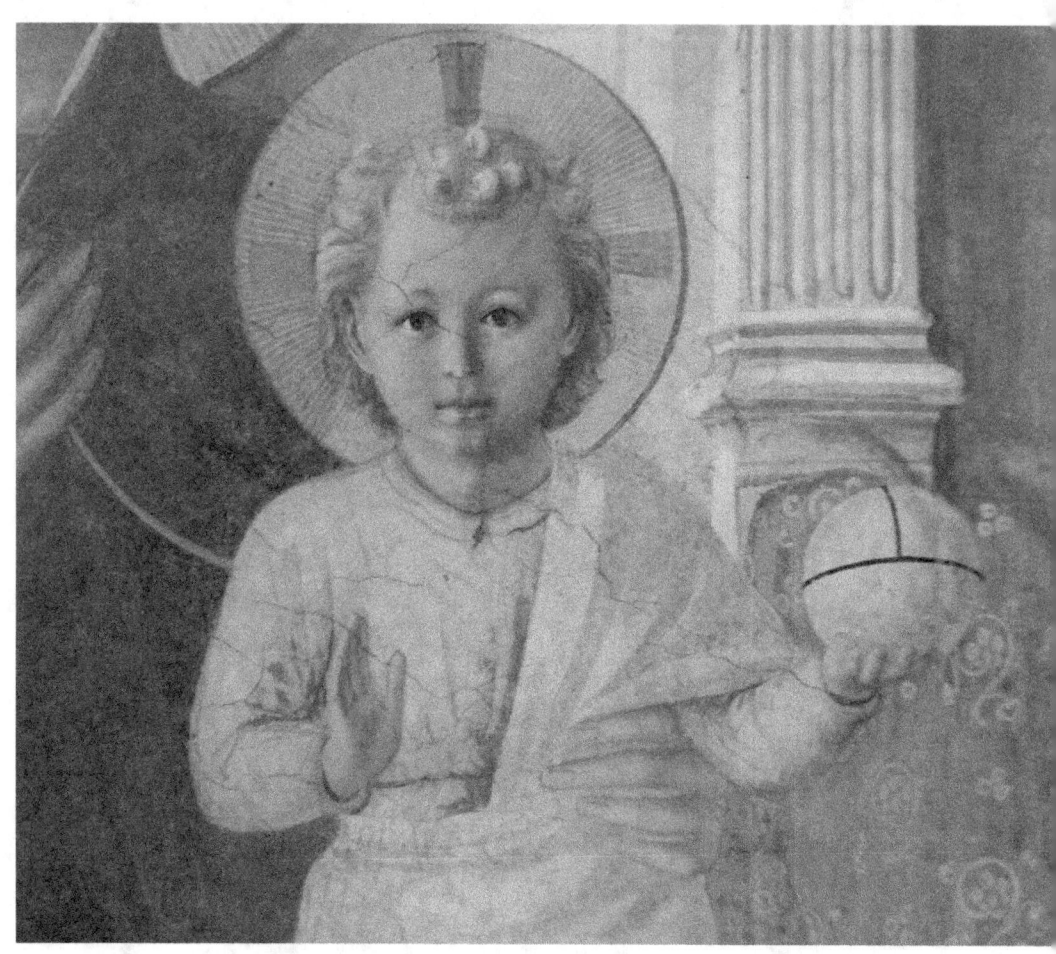

Fra Angelico, Virgin and Child Enthroned, c. 1450, detail, San Marco

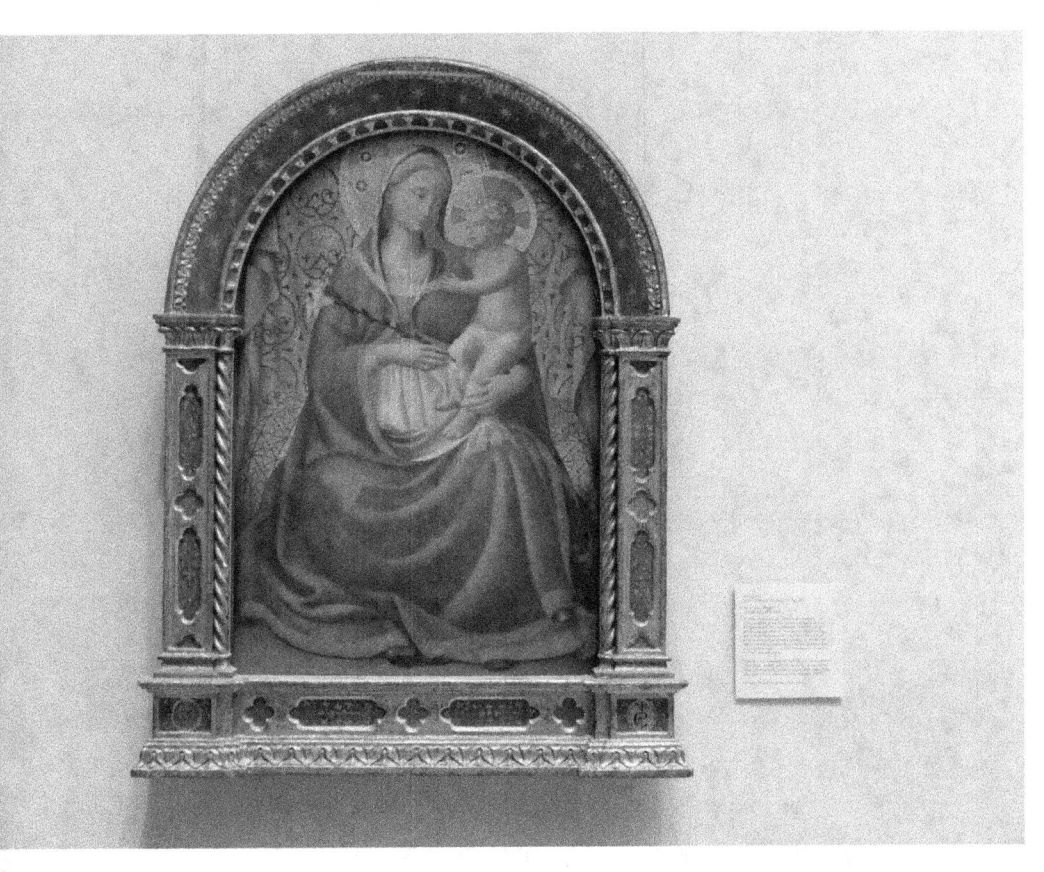

Fra Angelico, Madonna and Child, Metropolitan Museum of Art, New York

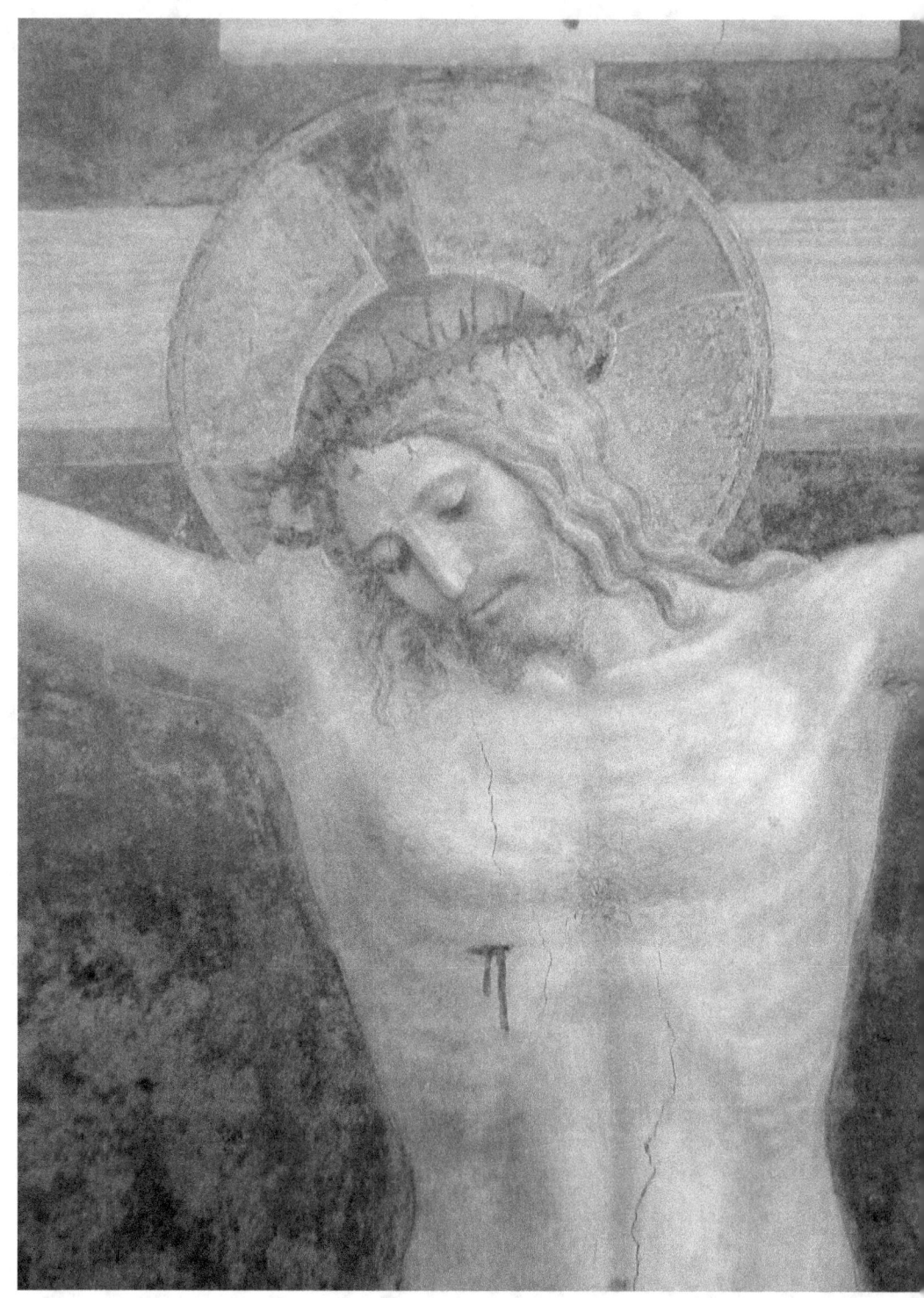

Fra Angelico, Christ On the Cross, c. 1442, detail, San Marco

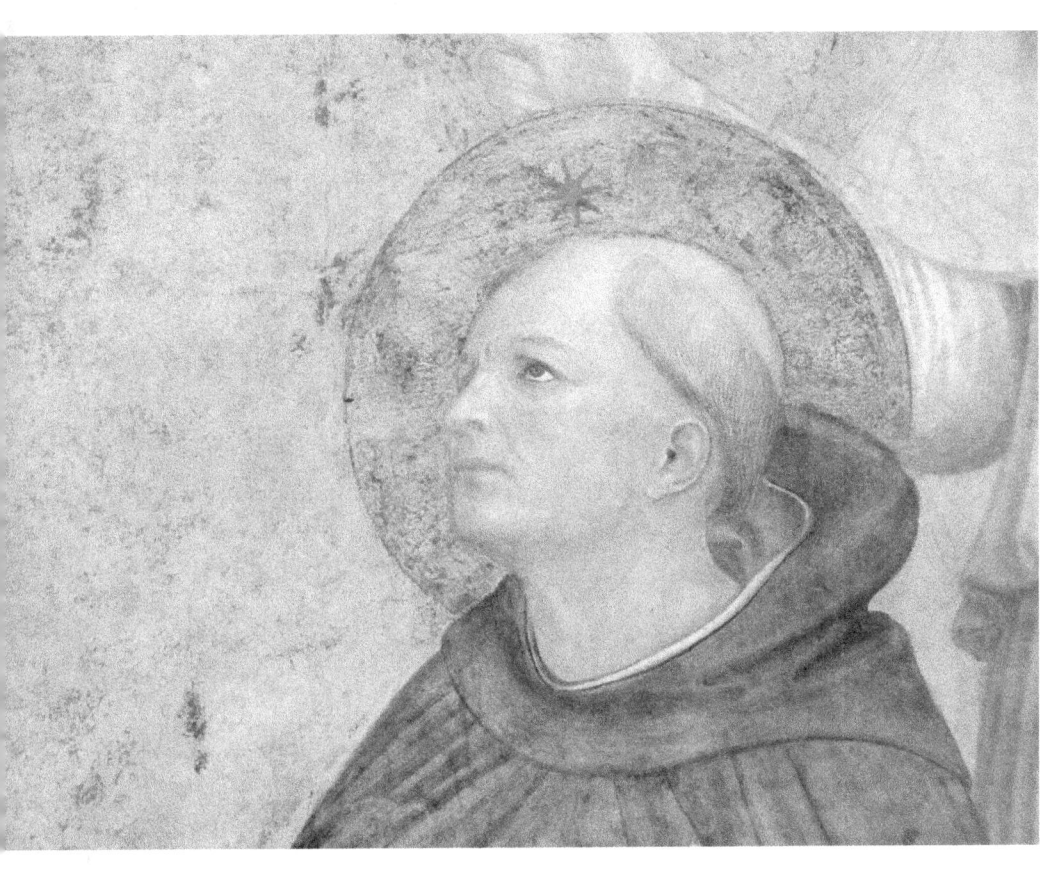

Fra Angelico, Crucifixion, detail, 1441-42, San Marco

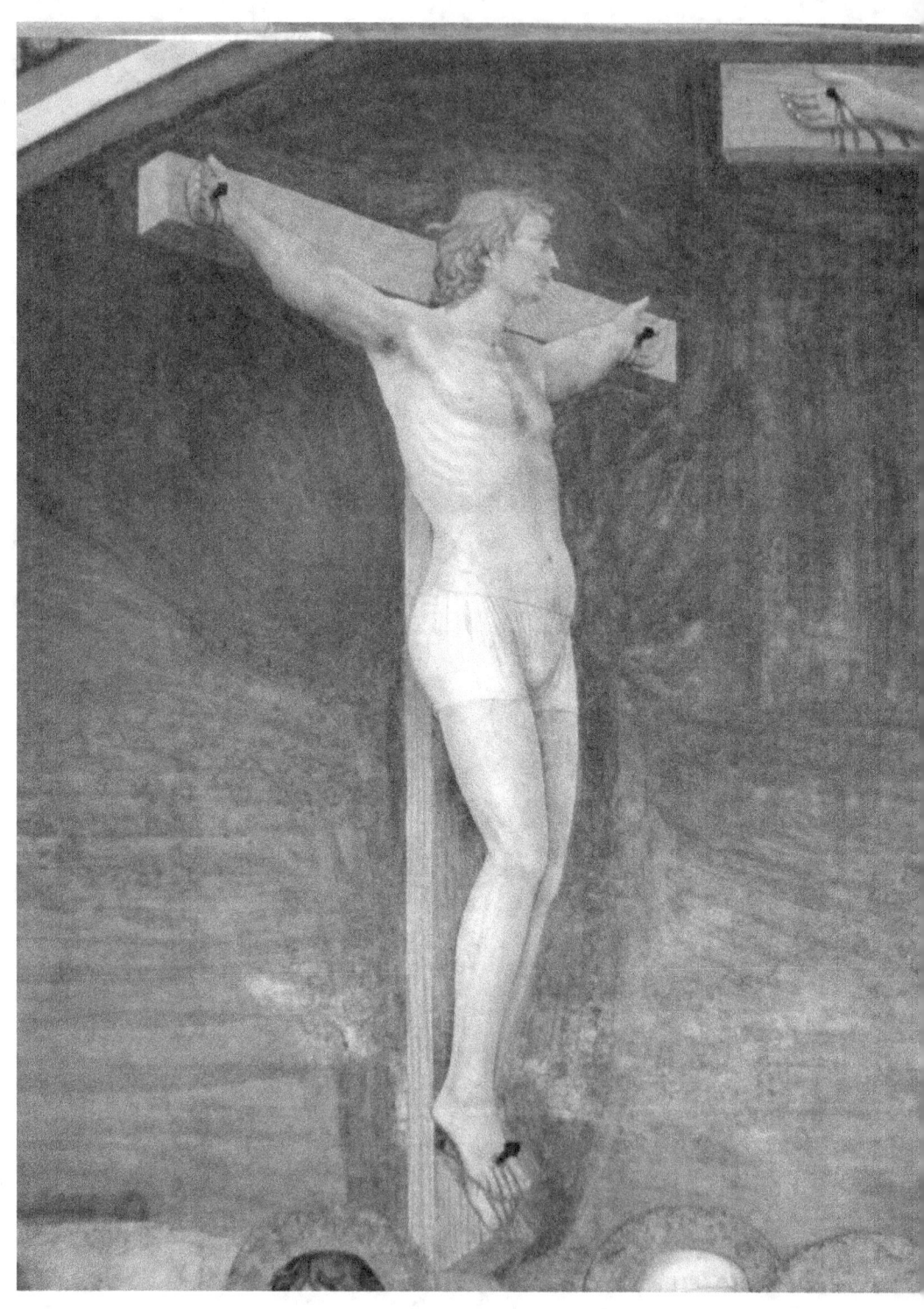

Fra Angelico, Crucifixion, 1441-42, San Marco, detail

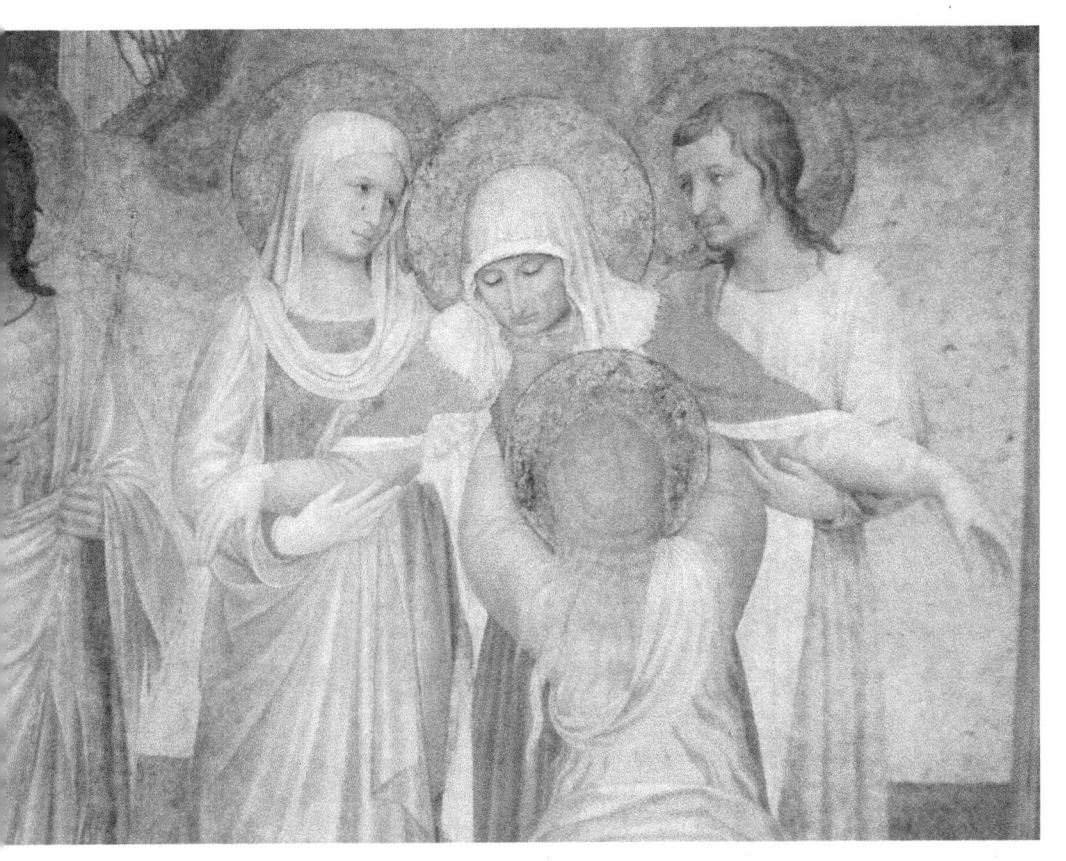

Fra Angelico, Crucifixion, detail

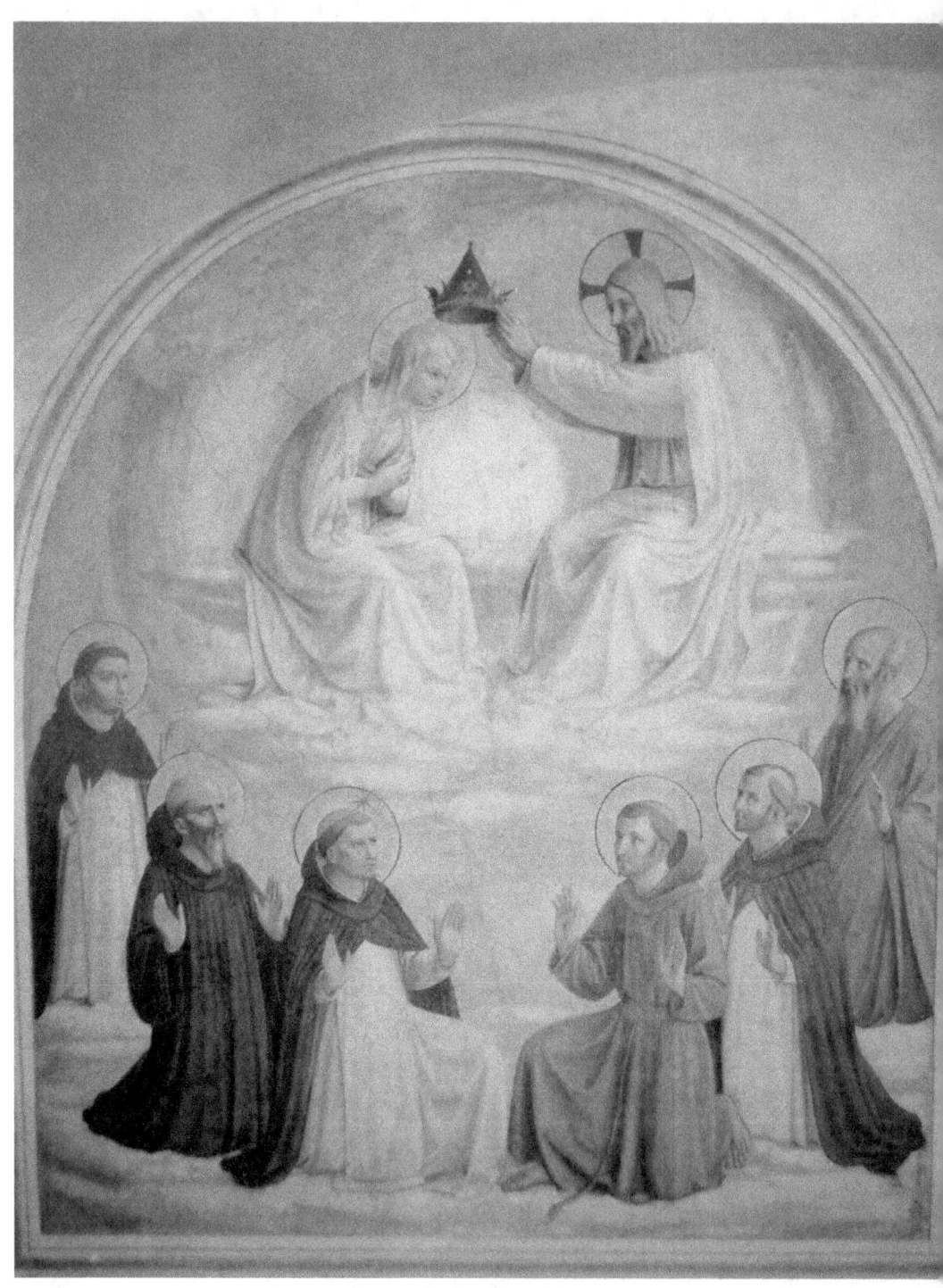

Fra Angelico, The Coronation of the Virgin, San Marco

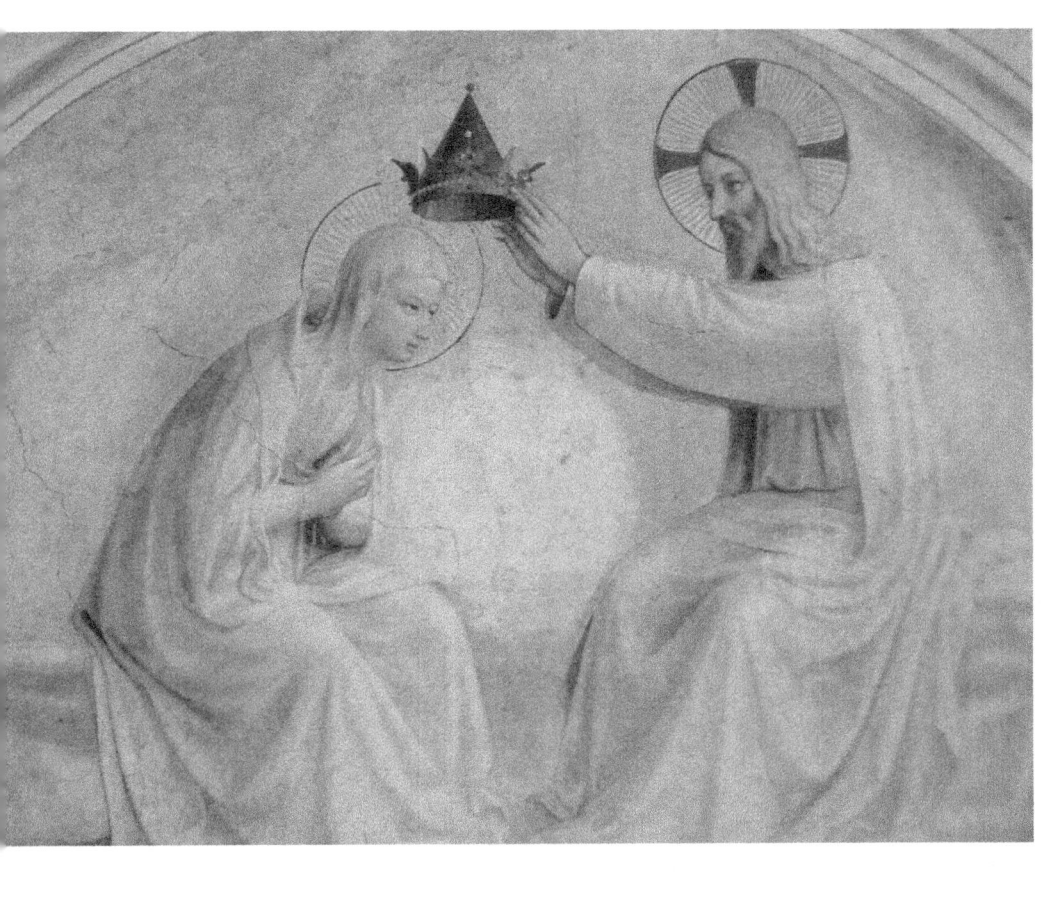

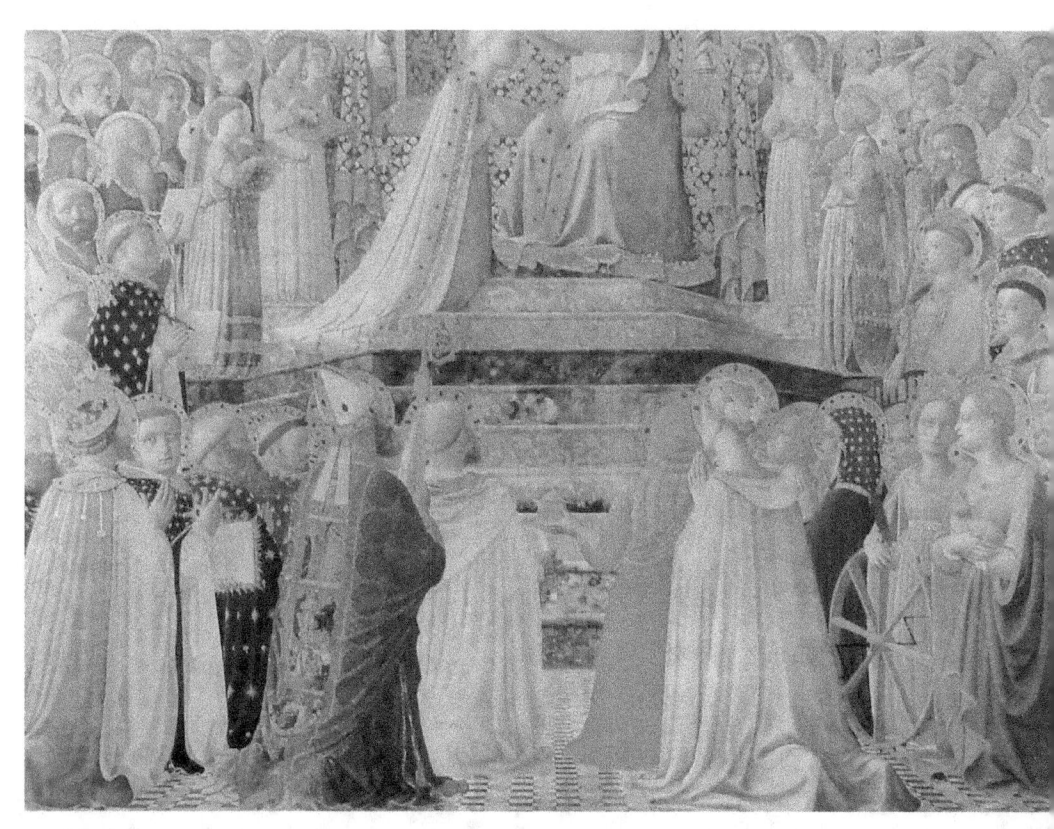

Fra Angelico, The Coronation of the Virgin, Louve, Paris, detail

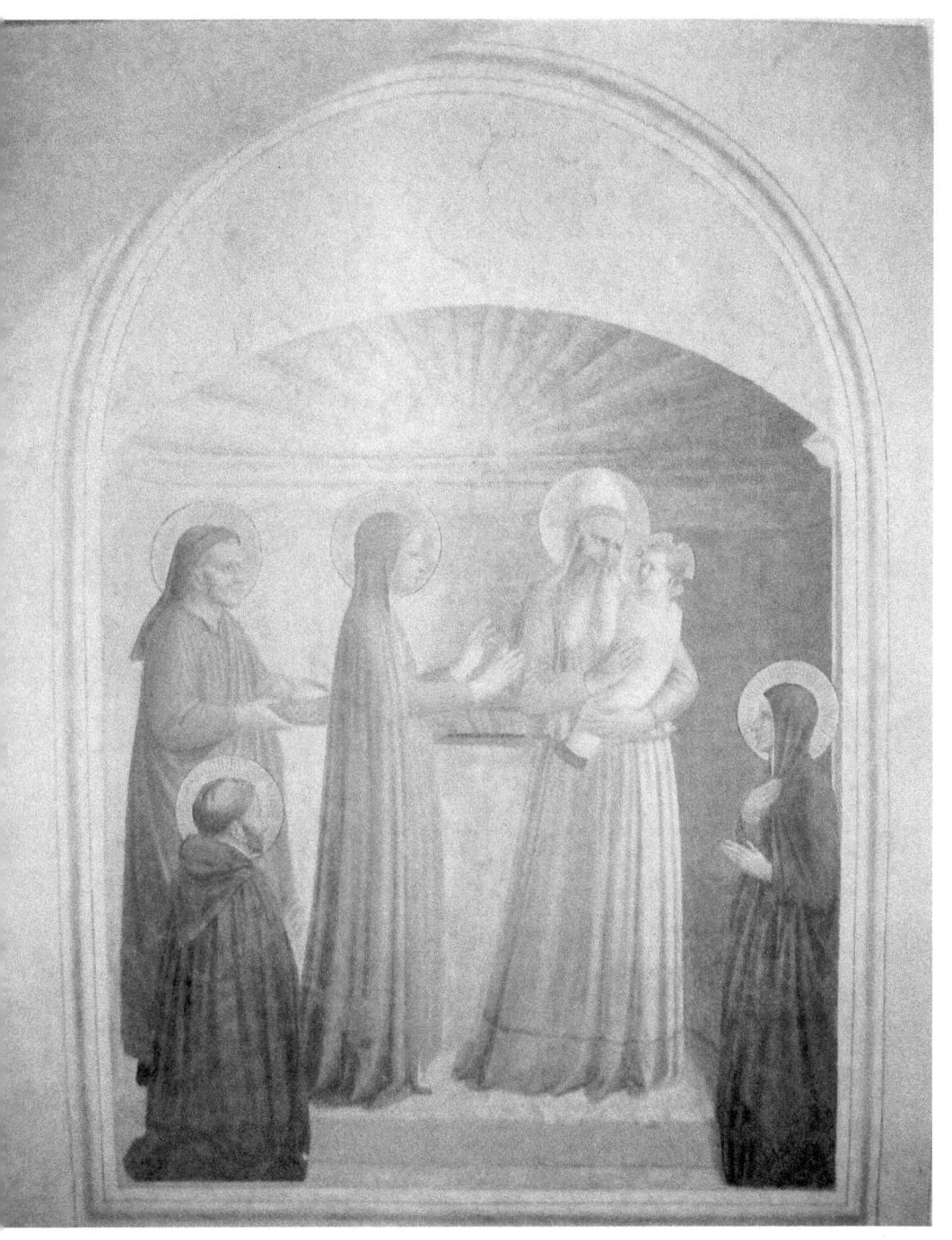

Fra Angelico, Presentation In the Temple, San Marco

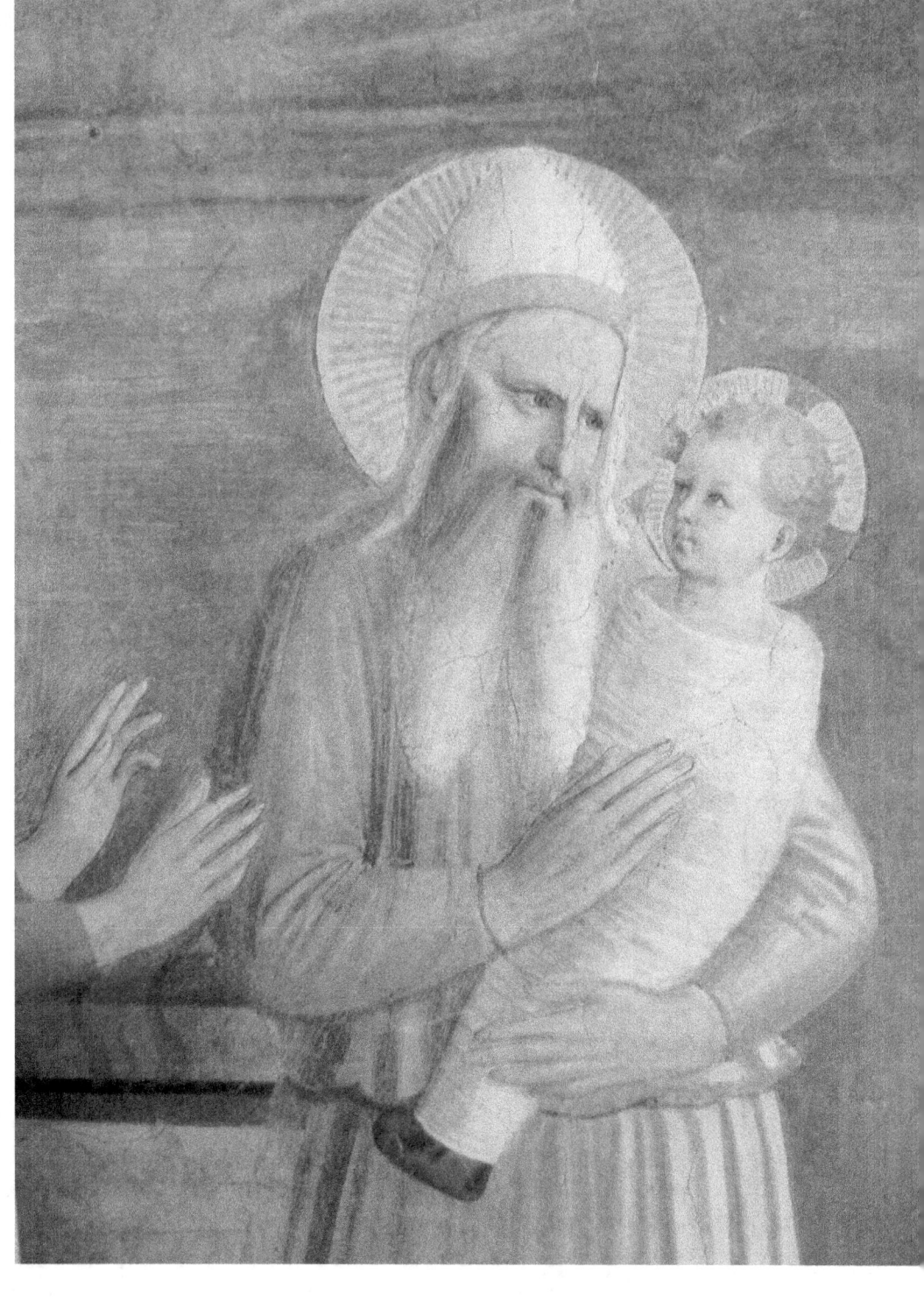

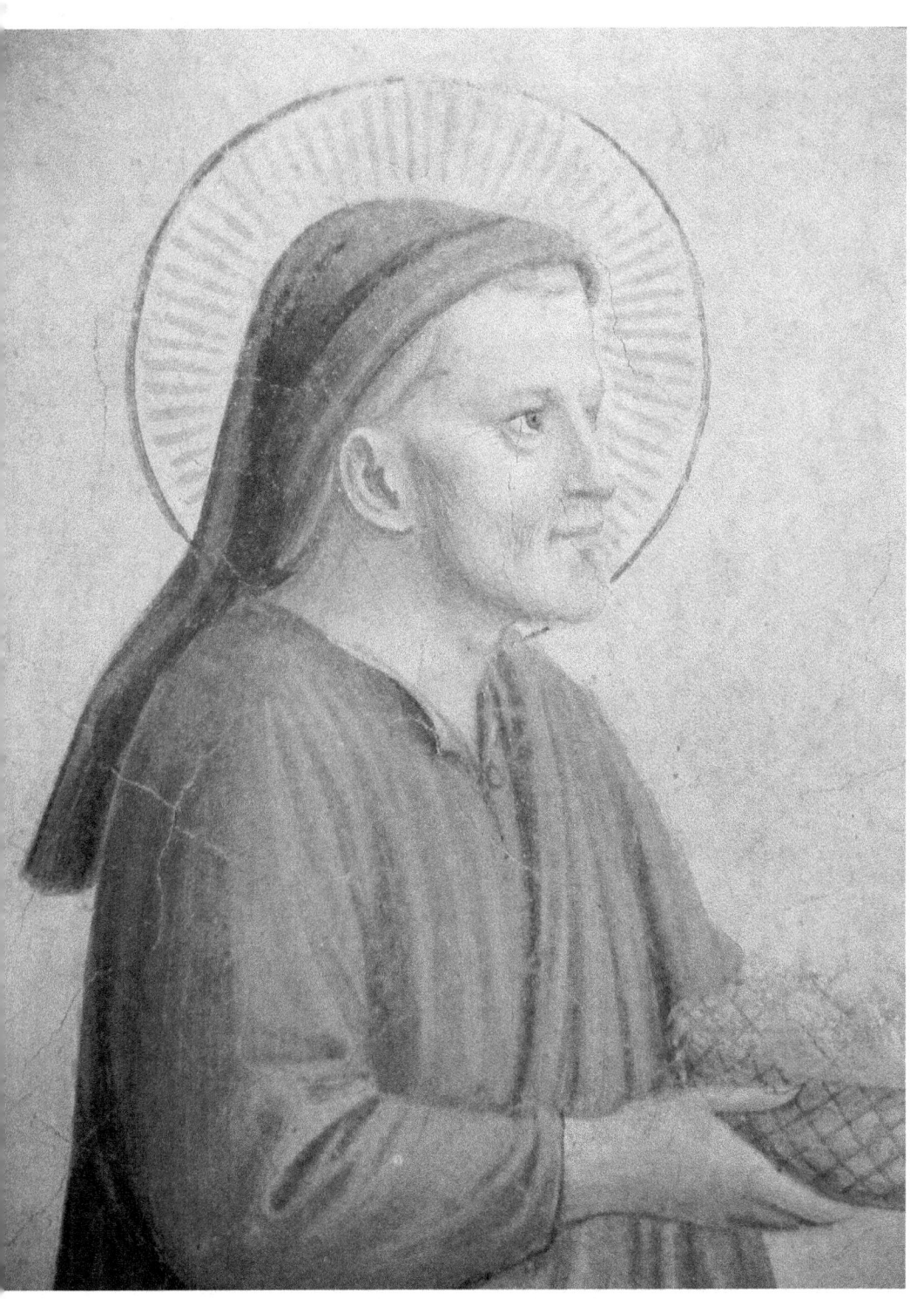

Fra Angelico, Presentation In the Temple, 1440-41, San Marco

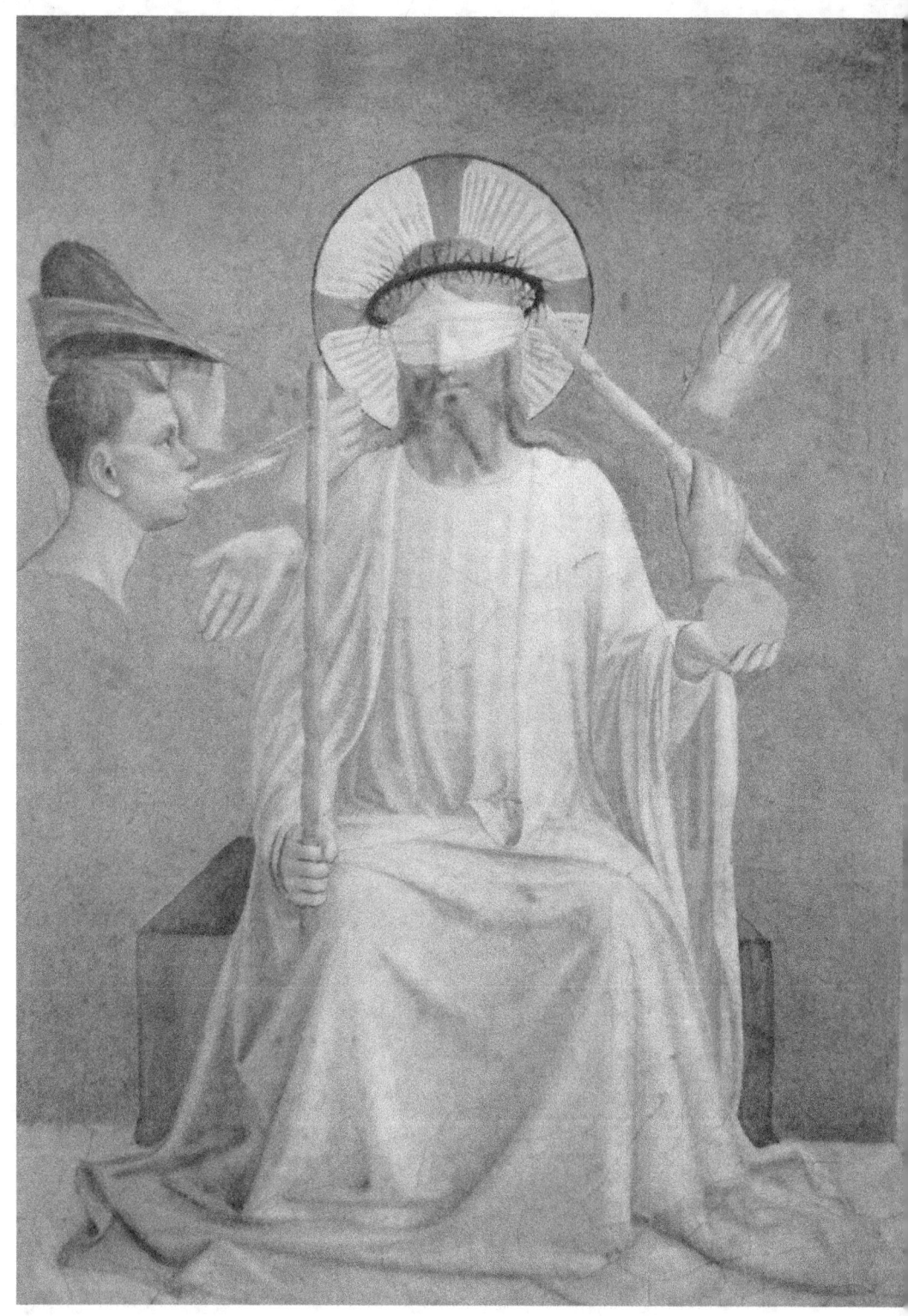

Fra Angelico, The Mocking of Christ, San Marco

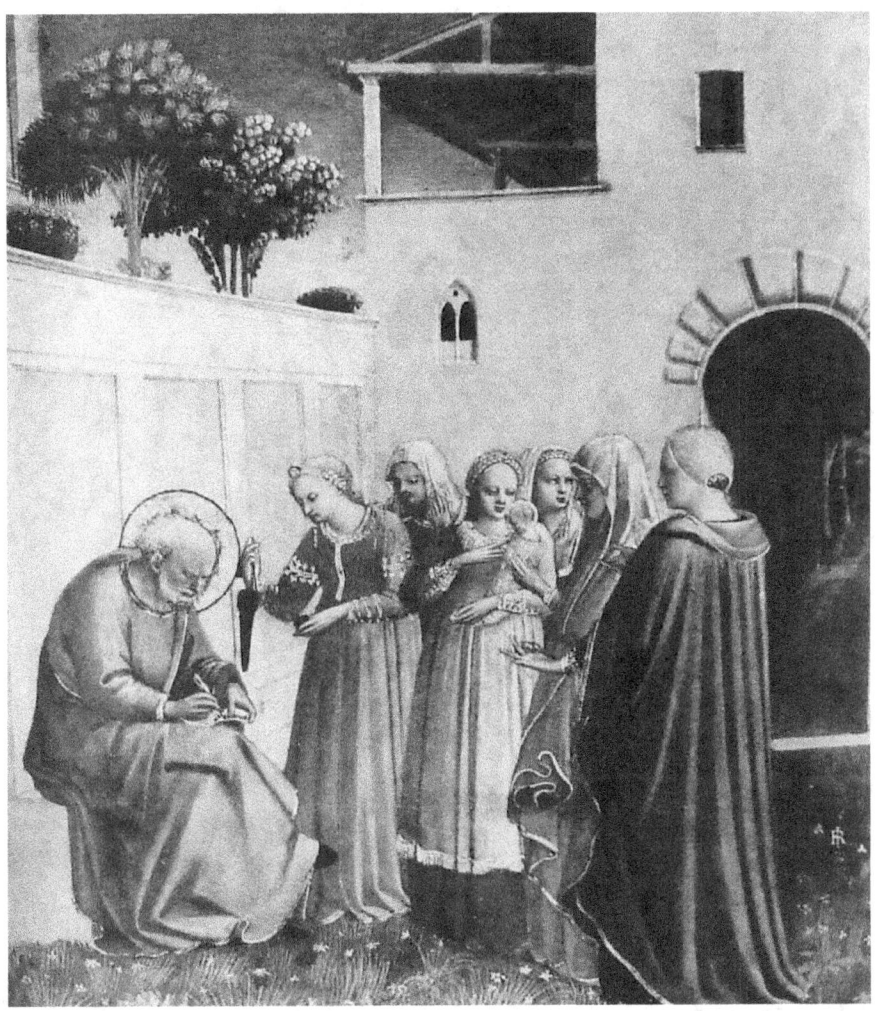

Fra Angelico, The Naming of John the Baptist, 1435

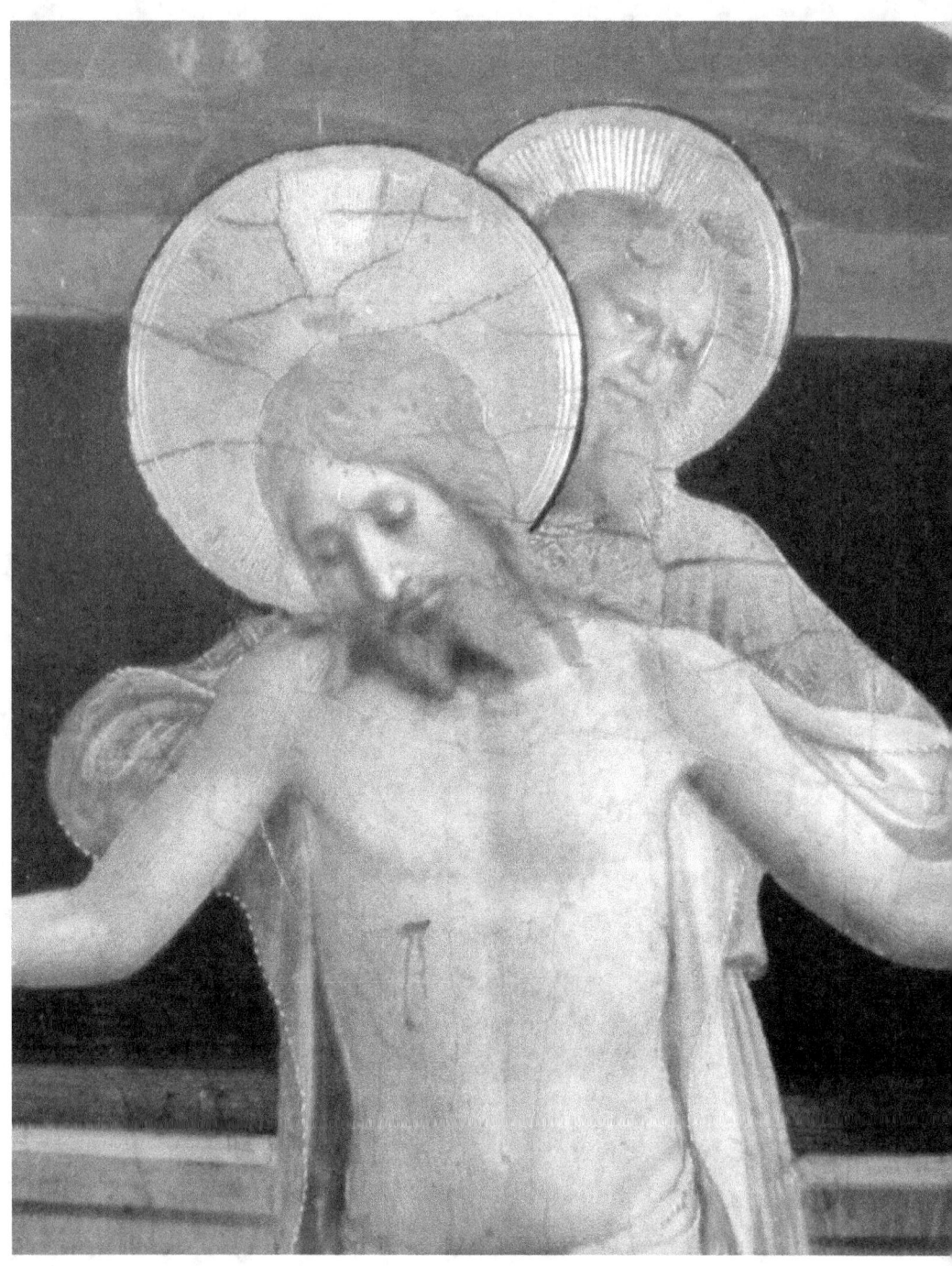

Fra Angelico, Lamentation Over the Dead Christ,
Alte Pinakothek, Munich, detail

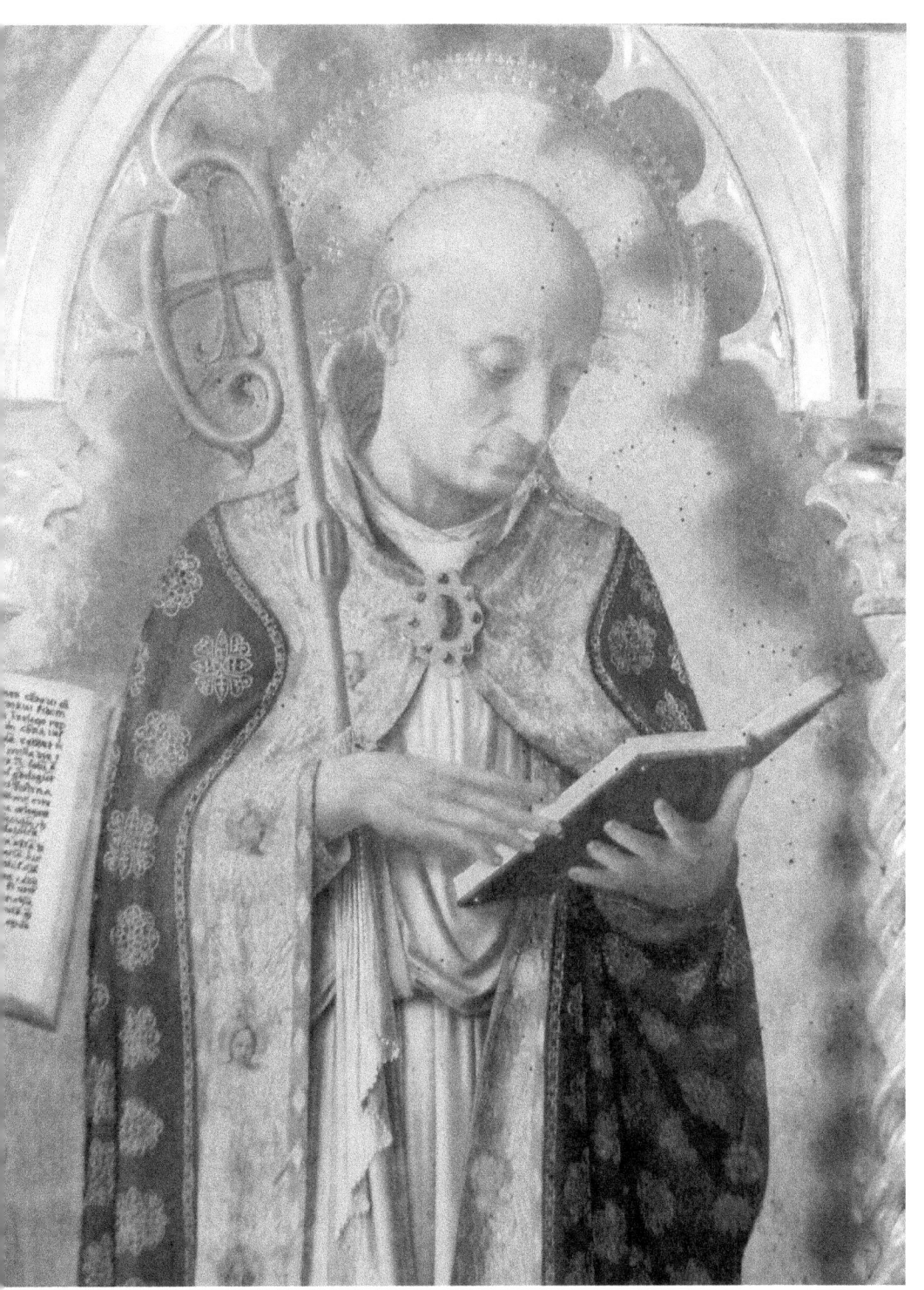

Fra Angelico, Perugia Altarpiece, 1448, detail

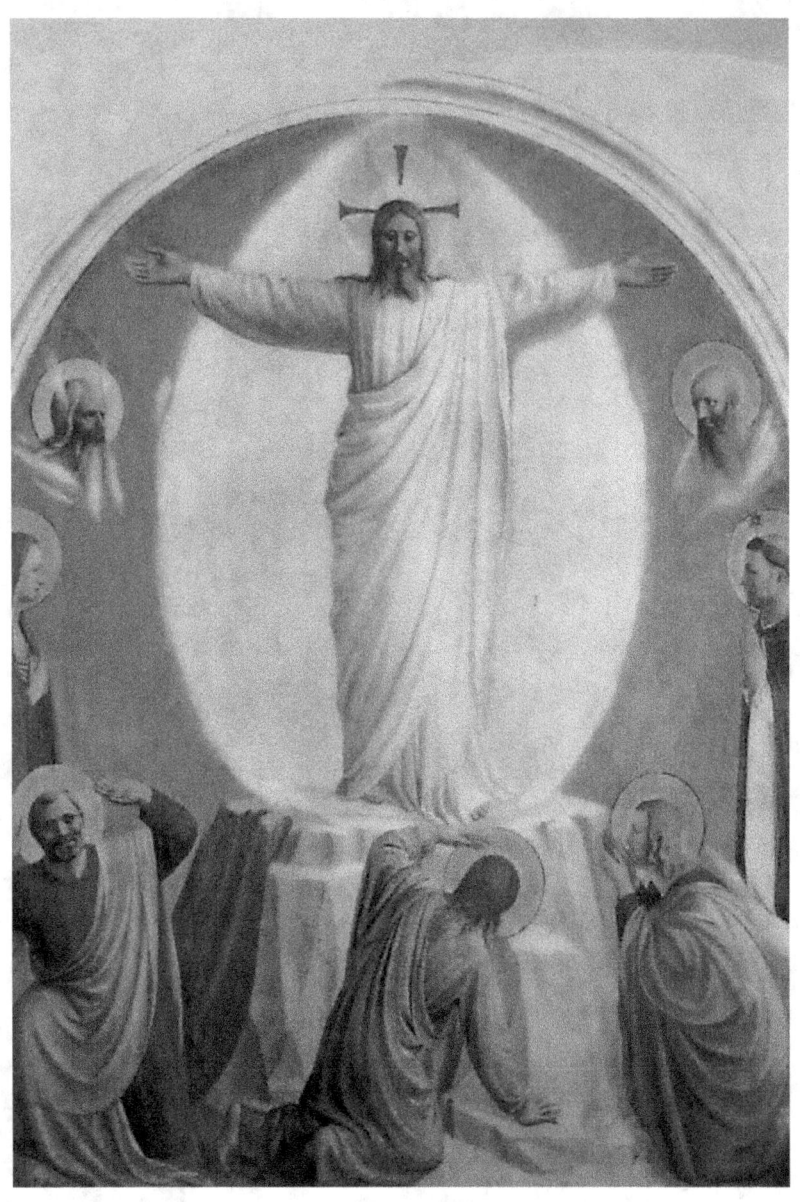

Fra Angelico, The Resurrection, San Marco, Florence

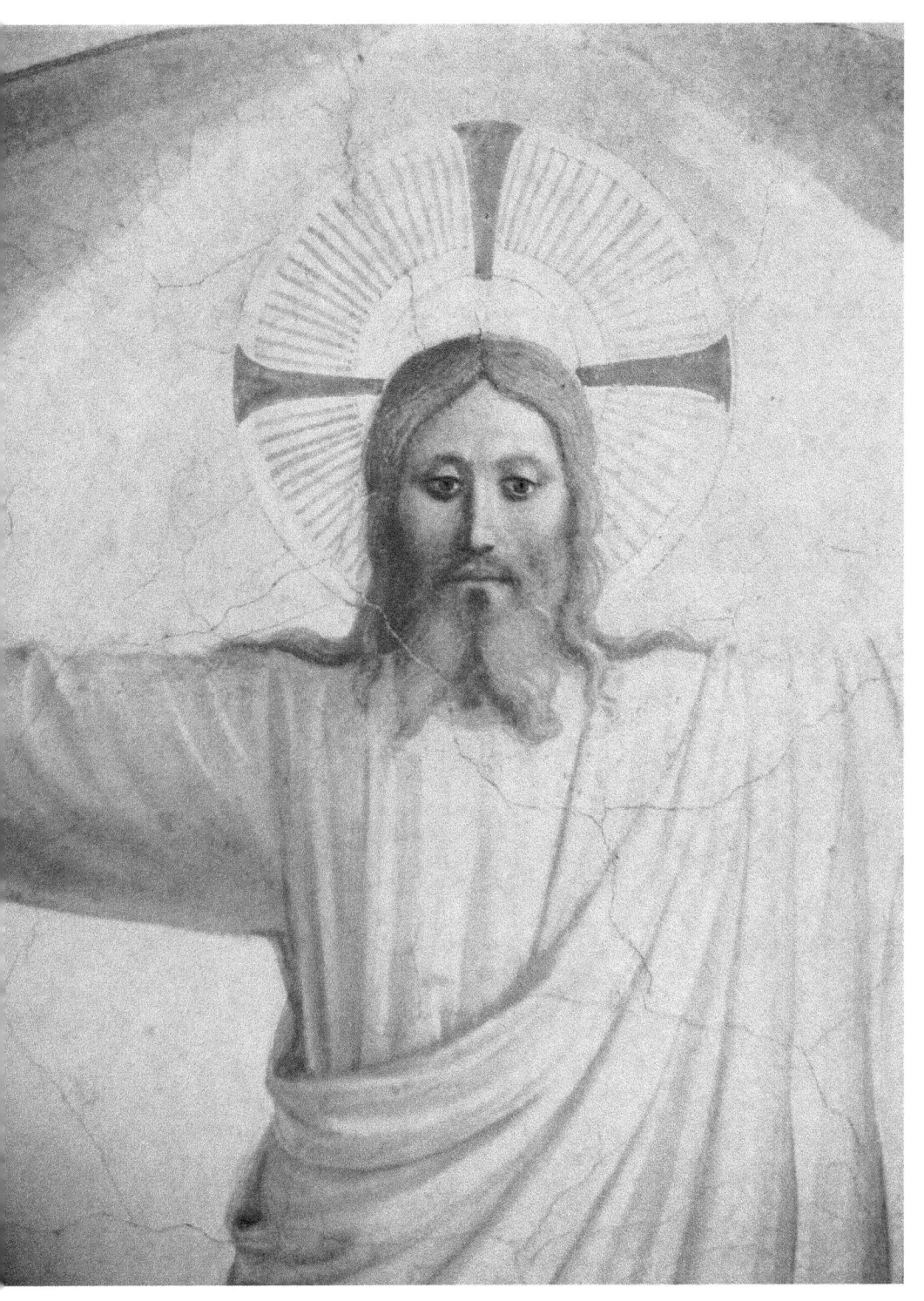

Fra Angelico, The Transfiguration, 1440-41, San Marco, detail

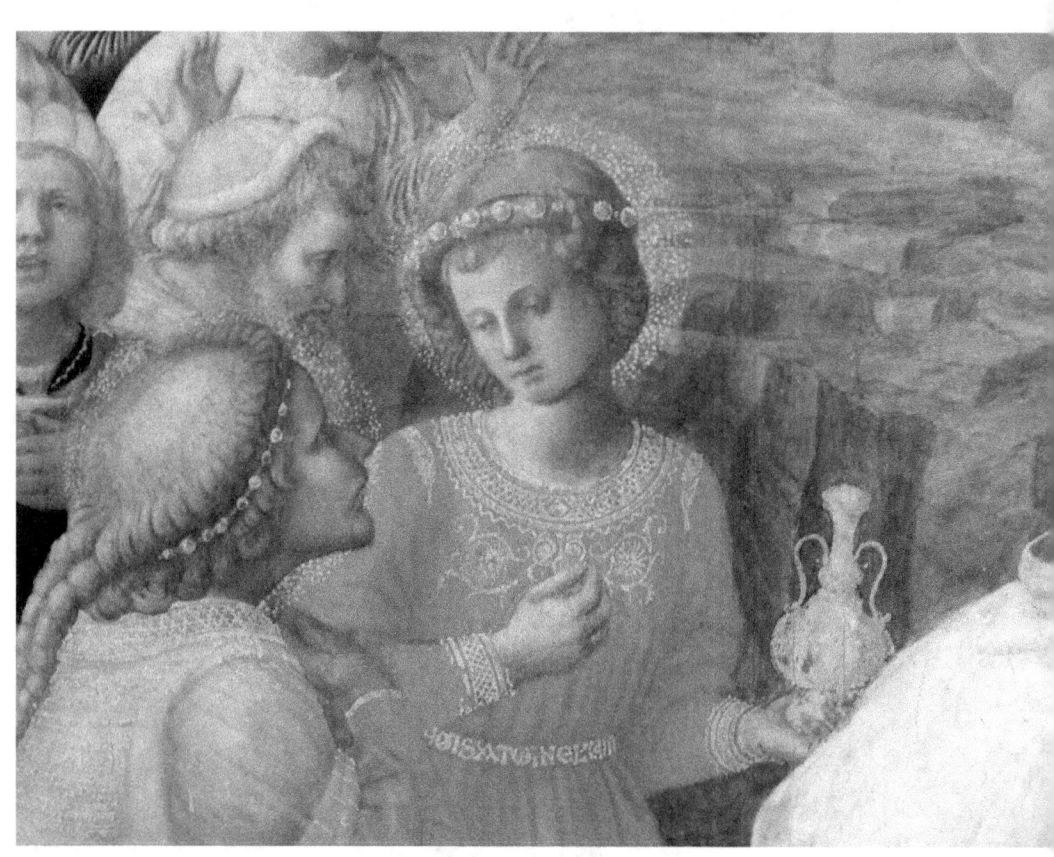

Fra Angelico, detail of Adoration of the Magi, 1445,
National Gallery of Art, Washington, DC (photo: author)

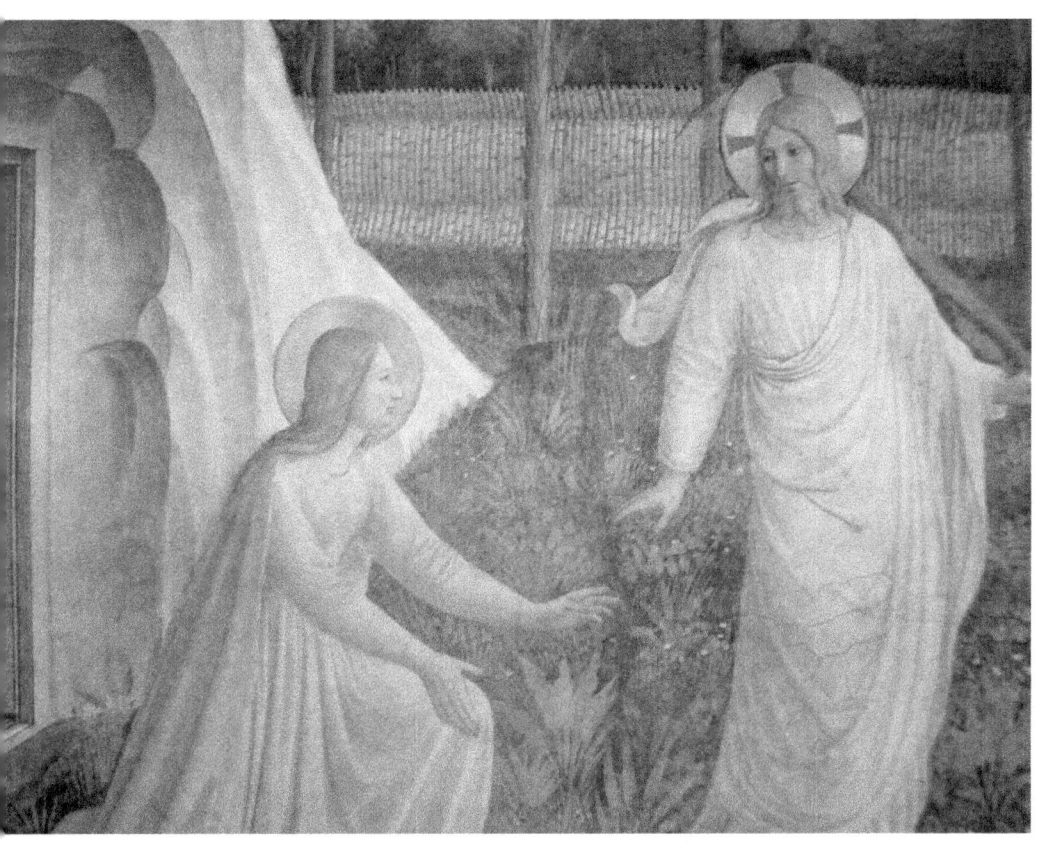

Fra Angelico, Noli Me Tangere

III

FRA ANGELICO AT FLORENCE

SAN MARCO

[1436-1445]

The church of San Giorgio – writes Vasari –

"had at this time been given to the monks of San Domenico da Fiesole,
but they did not occupy it longer than from about the middle of July
to the end of January, because Cosimo de' Medici and Lorenzo his
brother had obtained for them, from Pope Eugenius, the church and
convent of San Marco, which had previously been occupied by
Salvestrine monks, to whom San Giorgio was given in exchange.
Moreover, they (Cosimo and Lorenzo de' Medici), being much
devoted to religion, and zealous for the divine service and worship,
gave orders that the above-named convent of San Marco should be
entirely rebuilt according to the design and model of Michelozzo,
commanding that it should be constructed on the most extensive and
magnificent scale, with all the conveniences that those monks could
possibly desire."[*37]

And in the year 1436, the said monks made their entry with pomp and solemn fêtes, in which the three bishops of Taranto, Treves and Parentino, took part, preceded by the mace-bearers of the Signoria who were sent to give greater magnificence to the scene. Fra Cipriano, Vicar general of the new congregation of the "Osservanza," took possession of the convent in the name of that Order.[*38]

> "The first part completed," continues the Aretian biographer, "was that above the old refectory and opposite to the ducal stables, which had formerly been erected by the Duke Lorenzo de' Medici. In this place twenty cells were made, the roof was put on, and the various articles of wood-work brought into the refectory, which was finished as we see it in our day."[*39]
> [...]
> "The library was afterwards erected, it was vaulted above and below, and had sixty-four bookcases of cypress wood filled with the most valuable books. The dormitory which was in the form of a square, was next built, and finally the cloister was completed, with all the other truly commodious apartments of that convent, which is believed to be the most perfectly arranged, the most beautiful and most convenient building of its kind that can be found in Italy, thanks to the skill and industry of Michelozzo, who gave it up to its occupants entirely finished in the year 1452.[*40] Cosimo de' Medici is said to have expended 36,000 ducats on this fabric; it is added that while it was in course of construction, he gave the monks 366 ducats every year for their support."[*41]

In 1439, two years after the building was begun, the principal chapel was finished, and the work of restoring and embellishing the church was commenced. This was completed in 1441.

•

While the architect was engaged in restoring the church of San Marco, Fra Giovanni was probably commissioned to paint the altar-piece for the great altar. Vasari writes of it: "But exquisite and admirable above all is the picture of the High Altar in that church; for besides that the Madonna in this painting awakens devotional feeling in all who regard her, by the pure simplicity of her expression; and that the saints surrounding her have a similar character; the predella, in which are stories of the martyrdom of St. Cosmo, St. Damian, and others, is so perfectly finished, that one cannot imagine it possible for any thing to be executed with greater care, nor can figures more delicate, or more judiciously arranged, be conceived."[*42] Unfortunately the picture, now in the Academy of the Belle Arti, is in such bad condition that we are not able to confirm Vasari's judgment, for the tints have faded, in some parts leaving the undercolouring exposed, in others it is corroded even down to the white of the plaster ground work. The Virgin is enthroned, holding on her lap the child, whose right hand is uplifted to bless, while the left holds a globe. Beside the throne are groups of angels, in front on the right St. Dominic, St. Francis and St. Peter Martyr; on the left St. Laurence, St. Paul and St. Mark; above them kneel Sts. Cosmo and Damian, protectors of the Medici family, placed here in homage to the liberality of the Medici towards the Order.

In the predella, now divided, were represented various stories relative to the lives of Sts. Cosmo and Damian, which may be recognised in two little pictures (Nos. 257-258, Catalogue of 1893) at the Belle Arti, and in those now at the Gallery at Munich (Nos. 989, 990, 991). In the first of the two at Florence, the saints have cut off the leg of a sick man, and placed that of a negro in its stead. In the second is represented their burial together with the brethren. In those at Munich the scenes are:– the saints constrained by the judge Lisia to sacrifice to idols; the saints thrown into the sea and saved by angels, while the judge is liberated from two demons by their prayers; and lastly their crucifixion, while stones and arrows are aimed against them, but rebound on the executioners.[*43] Other similar subjects are represented in six "stories" divided into two panels (No. 234, Catalogue of 1893) in the Belle Arti. In the first the saints are seen exercising the healing art without receiving payment; they cure Palladia, who in her gratitude prays St. Damian in the name of God to accept a gift, her brother being wrathful not knowing the cause. In the second the judge Lisia obliges the saints and their three brethren to sacrifice to idols; in the third the angels save them from drowning; in the fourth they are condemned to be burnt alive, and sing psalms in the midst of the flames; in the fifth is the stoning; and lastly the decapitation.

These works, however, do not always show equal execution, therefore we might judge that the artist sometimes availed himself of the hand of an assistant.

From the records remaining to us, it does not appear that Fra Giovanni worked at any other pictures for his church, so it is probable he gave all his attention to adorning the convent, which on account of the works he has left there, may fairly be considered one of the finest monuments of Italian art.

•

It was not the first time that Fra Angelico had painted large mural frescoes. As he had already shown at Fiesole his mastery in that more minute style, which was to find more complete expression in the Roman pictures, so the convent of San Marco gave him scope to prove his genius also in this freer branch of art. In the cloisters, the corridors, the cells, and the rooms in which the monks met together, we find specimens of his artistic work, and in these various pictures all his favourite personages reappear one by one in larger proportions, but without losing that original grace and sentiment with which his smaller works are imbued. Indeed these show that he had studied from the life with independence and sincerity of purpose, and could render it with greater facility and decision.

A very noteworthy change in the character of Fra Angelico's art may be observed in these mural paintings. He must have perceived, after painting the tabernacle for the Linen Weavers' Guild, that a deeper study of the real was necessary to give life to his figures, especially when these should assume larger proportions.

To give intelligent expression even to dreams, visions and ideality of thought, a material and technical part is necessary; the mind may wander free in fantasy, through indefinite space, but it needs a firm hand to render the conception evident; and the clearer the expression is, the greater ability in the creation of his works does it show in the artist. Thus Fra Angelico, placing his figures in ideal surroundings, believed at first that refined thought was sufficient to make a perfect picture, and he illuminated his little figures with superficial delicacy, surrounding them with azure and gold, and so idealized them that they are more like diaphanous apparitions than human beings.

But he soon learned that by merely enlarging these little pictures, he could not succeed in giving them even that individuality to which he was led by natural taste and mode of life. In fact, what a difference lies between the figures of the Linen Weavers' Tabernacle painted in 1433, and those of the picture in the church of San Marco done in 1438! The first: void, weak and without expression; the second: full of life and character; and note that this difference strikes the eye even now, notwithstanding the difficulty of comparison owing to the wretched condition to which the panel at San Marco is reduced. In this cloister, therefore, where the pictures assume larger proportions and more importance, and the figures greater character and individuality of form, more solidity of artistic execution, – it is here we perceive that far as he still was from the world and worldly things, yet with earnest study and thought he had not failed to avail himself of the progressive development of art around him to improve his style and give more grandeur to his design.

We do not know whether the cause which influenced his mind was, that in coming down to Florence from the Fiesole cloister he was brought into more immediate contact with other styles of art, and artists who followed a different, even opposite method. The distance of his convent from the city was not, however, so great as to have prevented his visiting the immortal works which enriched Florence, or to diminish the relations of friendship or acquaintance which he surely had formed with his greater colleagues. In fact, Fra Angelico and Ghiberti must have already consulted together about the Tabernacle of the Linen

Guild; and the works which the pious monk sent from Fiesole to the churches and convents of Florence could not have been unknown there, any more than the works of the other artists in the city were to him.

Certain changes independent of external causes sometimes take place naturally, we might say spontaneously, in strong artistic temperaments. Fra Angelico felt and understood as he continued his work, that something was wanting in him before he could succeed in giving reality to his thoughts and sentiment; he necessarily perfected his studies, and investigated truth more conscientiously – the result was the new style, a natural consequence of artistic individual progress.

•

Opposite the entrance in the pretty cloister of the Florentine convent we may admire the figure of the crucified Christ who turns His eyes to St. Dominic kneeling below, and embracing the cross with both hands, while raising his head to meet the glance of the Saviour. In the five lunettes of the doors in the cloister, Fra Angelico has represented St. Peter Martyr, St. Dominic, Christ issuing from the sepulchre, Christ in the dress of a pilgrim, and St. Thomas Aquinas. The figure of the crucified Saviour is nobly beautiful in its simple and intelligent outline, firm design and life-like colouring. That of St. Peter Martyr is full of character; it is a half figure holding with his left hand the palm of martyrdom and a book which he rests on his side; the first finger of the right hand is placed on his mouth, indicating the silence of the cloister. St. Dominic has the book of his rules in one hand and the discipline, or rope for scourging in the other, as though to demonstrate that both moral and material influence should govern a religious community. The "Christ of the resurrection" shows His wounds, and St. Thomas Aquinas holds his book of theology in both hands.

In the arch of the hospice the painter has represented two Dominicans welcoming Christ, to remind the brethren that to offer hospitality to the poor and the pilgrims, was the same as receiving Christ.

The Redeemer with his hat hanging behind His shoulders leans on His pilgrim's staff; one of the brethren presses His left hand, and taking Him by the right arm invites Him to rest. The heads of the two devotees are full of character and expression, and on their faces beam the joy and love they feel for their unexpected guest. The second monk who clasps the Saviour's arm with both hands as though he can scarcely believe his own eyes, is drawn with such natural feeling that nothing greater can be desired or attained. Equally beautiful is the pilgrim Christ with His long beard and curls flowing on His shoulders; the whole scene in fact is given with great nobility and exquisite grace.

•

In the chapter-house of the convent Fra Angelico repeated the scene of the Crucifixion. Vasari writes of it thus: "Fra Giovanni was so greatly beloved for his admirable qualities by Cosimo de' Medici, that the latter had no sooner completed the church and convent of San Marco, than he caused the good father to paint the whole story of the Crucifixion of Jesus Christ on one of the walls of the chapter-house. In this work figures of all those saints who have been heads and founders of religious bodies, are mourning and bewailing at the foot of the cross on one side; and on the other, St. Mark the Evangelist beside the Mother of the Son of God, who has fainted at sight of the crucified Saviour. Around the Virgin are the Maries, who are sorrowing with and supporting her; they are accompanied by the saints Cosimo and Damian.

"Beneath this work, in a frieze above the dado the master executed a figure of St. Dominic standing at the foot of a tree; on the branches of which are medallions, wherein are all the popes, cardinals, bishops, saints, and masters in theology who had belonged to Fra Giovanni's Order of the Preaching Friars, down to his own day."[*44]

In this masterly work Fra Angelico pours out with full hands the most vivid and intense feelings of his soul, and if he does not attain to grand dramatic power, he at least succeeds in depicting with rare ingenuity the varied expressions of sorrow, despair, hope and faith which animate each person, and in giving natural and life-like character and attitude to the various heads.

The group of the fainting Virgin may possibly seem conventional, but what sweet piety is in the feeling of the other figures! St. Dominic, devoutly kneeling, inclines his head (cleverly foreshortened and marvellously expressed) and extends his arms to the Redeemer; St. Zenobi (or St. Ambrose the archbishop) standing upright, points with his right to the Saviour; St. Jerome, in hermit's dress, bends forward and clasps his hands in prayer; St. Augustine holds his pen in one hand, his book and pastoral staff in the other; St. Francis brings his hand to his brow in an attitude of melancholy indefinable sadness. The Saints Benedict, Bernard and Romuald follow, then St. Thomas Aquinas with a most beautiful head full of life and character (it must certainly be a portrait, so life-like is the expression), next St. Peter Martyr with his hands on his breast; and lastly in the foreground an unknown monk (Padre Marchese thinks it is St. John Gualbert) who weeps, with his left hand over his eyes.[*45]

On the left of the fresco, near the swooning Virgin, stands St. John Baptist pointing to the Saviour; St. Mark kneeling shows his gospel; St. Laurence clasps his hands on his breast; and St. Cosmo wrings his hands as he contemplates the Cross; while St. Damian turns, covering his eyes, and weeping the mournful loss of the Lord.

In the ornamentation of the simulated frame which surrounds the fresco, are hexagonal spaces containing half figures of prophets with labels, containing texts referring to the passion of Christ; and below them on the right, the Erythrean Sibyl. In the lower part of the frieze, are ten rounds, containing portraits of the most illustrious members of the Dominican Order. In the centre St. Dominic, on the left Pope Innocent V., Cardinal Ugone, Father Paulo the Florentine, the Archbishop St. Antonino (this must surely have been added later), the blessed ones Giordano of Saxony, Niccolò, Remigius the Florentine and Buoninsegna the martyr. On the right are the blessed brethren John Dominici, Peter of the Marshes, Albertus Magnus, St. Raymond, Chiaro of Sesto, St. Vincent Ferreri and Bernard the martyr.

Retouches and restorations are not wanting in this picture, the drapery has been repainted in several parts and the background has been smudged with that reddish colour, which, in altering the tone of the whole fresco, has injured the limpidity of colour and original refinement of harmony.

•

The chronicles of the convent of San Marco record another Crucifixion by Fra Angelico in the refectory of the monks, "probably," writes Padre Marchese, "a replica of that which he had already painted in the Fiesolan convent." This now no longer exists, it appears to have been destroyed to make space for Sogliani's great fresco of St. Dominic at table with his brethren, when they were supplied with bread by angels. But in the cells and dormitories of the Florentine convent Fra Angelico scattered lovely proofs of his genius and sentiment, pouring out on them with rare talent the most exquisite grace of his brush, and tenderest thoughts of his soul. From the "Annunciation" to the various scenes from the life of Christ; from the "Virgin among the saints," in the corridor, to the decoration of the room which Cosimo had built for himself in his favourite convent, all breathe such sweet poesy in the grace and simplicity of the varied scenes, that one cannot look at them unmoved.

•

Facing the entrance of the upper corridor of the cloister he painted the Angel bringing the glad tidings to the Virgin. We have already noted in regard to this subject as created by him at Cortona, how the representation finds its greater development here, where the artist succeeds better in rendering the feeling of veneration on the part of the heavenly messenger, and the submissive humility of the Virgin. The same subject is repeated in a cell (No. 3), but in this design, which breathes the same sentiment of sweetness and piety, St. Dominic in reverent attitude is looking on.

•

On the wall at the left of the entrance is a Crucifixion, with St. Dominic on his knees, embracing the cross, the figures are about half life size, the design similar to that which we have already seen in the cloister, but showing less ability. Nor are these the only Crucifixions which our artist painted. He has reproduced the subject in several cells, always varying either the attitude of the Saviour, or the persons who adore Him, but the serene attitude of the Son of God is unalterable. Without exaggerated contractions or violent action He remains fixed on the cross, His head bowed in mute contemplation of the figures below Him. These, on the contrary, are the prey of sorrow and despair, they cover their faces, or weep distractedly at His feet.

Some of these frescoes of the Crucifixion with St. Dominic kneeling below, may be classed as decidedly by other hands, the execution being weak, the drawing incorrect, and the sentiment inefficiently expressed. These variants are doubtless attributable to the assistants he employed in their execution.

In the fresco representing the *Noli me tangere* Angelico gives us a work full of freshness and life, idealized in Giottesque style. The figure of Christ is majestic, as with a sign He withdraws Himself from the kneeling Magdalene, who supplicatingly extends her arms towards Him.

Most lovely are the composition and feeling of the figures in the "Nativity," where the Virgin and St. Joseph with joined hands kneel in adoration of the Babe stretched on a heap of straw on the ground. A little above, on the right stands St. Dominic, and behind the Virgin on the left a female saint kneels, her hands clasped in prayer. In the background beneath a humble shed are the bull and the ass, and four adoring angels above.

In the "Transfiguration on Mount Tabor" the figure of the ascending Christ with outstretched arms and noble features is one of Fra Angelico's best works, but the attitudes of the Apostles are conventional; the kneeling figure on the left with hands upraised to express confusion and surprise at the resurrection, is too mannered, and by its pose and action disturbs the serene harmony of the picture.

•

In the "Institution of the Holy Sacrament," Fra Angelico, in true Giottesque style, represented the Apostles at the mystic feast, and Christ giving them the consecrated wafer, while He holds the chalice in His left hand. Here the figures of the disciples admirably express varied feelings of devotion and joy in receiving the divine food from the hand of the Master. But the fresco which surpasses all, in nobility of line and simple grandeur of conception, is the "Coronation of the Virgin."

Christ and the Virgin are seated in glory above the light clouds, the Son places the celestial crown on the head of the Mother who humbly bows her whole form towards Him, with hands crossed on her bosom. Her face is irradiated by an ineffable and heavenly smile, the supreme expression of happiness; the drapery of both is white and delicate, enveloping the limbs with well defined folds.

The figures without being ineffectual, indeed they are even forcible, yet appear aerial apparitions, and veritable visions of divinity. Six saints in ecstasy assist at the triumph, St. Thomas Aquinas, St. Paul, St. Dominic, St. Francis, St. Peter Martyr and St. Benedict, three on the right and three on the left, in a semicircular composition, all in attitudes of contemplative ecstasy.

The frescoes of the Maries at the Sepulchre, may also be considered one of our artist's masterpieces. The risen Christ emerges to half His figure from the clouds which envelop Him, while the holy women contemplate the empty sepulchre, and the angel seated in it points out the miracle which has happened. Other scenes worthy of notice are the "Presentation in the Temple," "Christ in Hades," and the "Buffeting of the Saviour," and "The Prayer in the Garden."

•

In one of the last cells, the "Crucifixion" is reproduced in a new manner, which represents Christ having ascended the ladder and offering Himself to death: His Mother faints at his feet in the arms of Mary Magdalene.

Marchese asserts that this composition was inspired by a legend of St. Mary Magdalene in the language of the 14th century. "And I thought that Messer Gesù, ascended the cross by a ladder voluntarily, offering His hands and feet. A centurion who was afterwards saved saw the deed, and like a wise man he said within himself, oh, what a marvel is here! that this prophet appears to willingly place himself on the Cross, neither murmuring nor resisting! And while he stood admiring, Messer Gesù had ascended sufficiently high, and turning on the ladder opened His kingly arms, and extended His hands to those who were waiting to nail them."[*46]

•

Lastly in the room which Cosimo de' Medici had prepared for his own use in the convent and where he often talked with the Prior Fra Antonino, Fra Angelico painted an "Adoration of the Magi." As Pope Eugene IV. slept in this room when he came to Florence in 1442 to assist at the consecration of the church, it is probable that this Adoration allusive to the Epiphany, at which time the consecration took place, was painted at that epoch.

The fresco, rich in figures and beauty, is executed with real mastery. The personages of the royal cortège vary in type and character, in expression and sentiment, showing the great pains our artist had taken in the painting of this important work, which now, unhappily restored and injured, only allows us to guess at the wonderful beauty with which it was once filled.

We see his own hand more completely in the fresco in the corridor representing the Virgin enthroned, with the child seated on her knee and several saints at the sides. On the right are St. Paul, St. Thomas Aquinas, St. Laurence, and St. Peter Martyr; on the left St. Mark, St. Cosmo and St. Damian, and St. Dominic, holding an open book where it is written: *Caritatem habete; humilitatem servate; paupertatem voluntariam possidete. Maledictionem*

Dei et meam imprecor possessiones inducenti in meo Ordine.

This painting, one of the most perfect in the convent, is one of Angelico's best, and shows what a high degree of ability he had reached. The gentle head of the Virgin bends down to look at her Son with the golden curls, whose face with sparkling eyes breathes an infantile grace. The execution is accurate, the figures well designed, full of character, nobility and life; the delicacy of tone, just balance of composition and freshness of colouring, are mingled with the most profound sentiment and intimate knowledge of truth.

Rio thinks this fresco was done while Fra Angelico was in Tuscany after 1450; his adieu, as it were, to his brethren; a last legacy to that devout household with whom he had shared joys and sorrows, and from which he was about to be separated. There is nothing to refute this; but it appears to us that he who had painted the great Crucifixion of the chapter-house might well have done at the same time this fresco. It is a compendium of all his technical qualities and feeling, and demonstrates how little by little he succeeded, while still preserving his own spirit, in reaching the real in art, and giving it life in a manner all his own. But in comparing the pictures of the chapel of Pope Nicholas V. in Rome, with this fresco, we cannot avoid noticing in those a greater freedom of composition and grouping of the figures, a greater majesty of design, a truth and depth of observation, not recognisable in any of his earlier works, nor even in the large Crucifixion, which is justly considered one of the pious monk's best works.

AT FLORENCE

IN THE GALLERY OF
ANCIENT AND MODERN ART

The enthusiasm aroused by Fra Angelico's pictures, caused a vivid desire amongst the various religious orders of the city, to possess some work of his; Dominicans, Vallombrosians, Chartreuse monks, and the Camaldolese of Santa Maria degli Angeli, vied with each other, and all in turn obtained some of his admirable creations.

Among the panels painted by Fra Giovanni for the Florentine churches and convents, the one which excels all for intensity of sentiment and sincerity of expression is the "Deposition from the Cross," once in the Sacristy of Santa Trinità, and now in the Ancient and Modern Gallery, a panel "in which," writes Vasari, "he put so much care that we may class it among the best things he ever did."

The disciples with loving reverence let down from the Cross, which occupies the centre of the composition, the body of the Saviour. His face, drooping on the left shoulder, breathes a sorrowful calm, and divine serenity which death itself could not destroy. The nude is intelligently rendered, in nobility of form, softness of line, and transparency and morbidity of colouring. On the left stands a group of women; St. Mary Magdalene kisses the feet of Christ; the Virgin contemplates Him in a trance of sadness; on the right the disciples discuss the melancholy drama among themselves, while below, a kneeling saint holds his right hand to his breast and extends the left in a sorrowful wonder. In the background is a hilly landscape with the Holy City on the left, and Mount Calvary which the artist "with poetic and devout conceit," writes Marchese, "has drawn adorned with grass and flowers, as though to denote that at the touch of the feet and precious blood of Jesus Christ, the bare heights were reclad in rich and verdant beauty. Although marred by restoration – for the eye is offended by the inharmonious contrast of tints, the effect of unskilful retouching, – we may consider this painting as one of the most beautiful works which Fra Angelico has left us. Grandeur and simplicity are marvellously blended with freshness of colour, and correctness of design with most intense expression and pure sentiment."

The landscape in the background shows the usual defects of perspective, but the mountains shade off delicately against the distant blue of the sky, the plain is illuminated with infinite flowerets, and a rich verdure clothes the summit of the sacred hill. In the pilasters of the frame are small figures of Saints, some of the best and finest that Fra Angelico ever painted, and in the gables above the three arches Lorenzo Monaco has represented the "Noli me tangere," the "Resurrection," and the "Maries at the Sepulchre."

Here the question naturally arises: Why should Lorenzo Monaco have limited his work solely to the three little scenes in the gables of the frame, while Fra Angelico has given us the beautiful little figures of the pilasters which show all his peculiar grace and refinement? Why did an artist capable of producing those admirable saints, leave to Fra Lorenzo Monaco the office (all the worse if he had been, as some say, his master) of finishing the work with only those three insignificant little scenes? And can we suppose that Fra Lorenzo Monaco, already at the apex of his fame, should accept, and, still more strange, be content with a secondary part in Fra Giovanni's work?

The answer is more simple than it at first appears. There is no doubt that the scenes in the Gothic gables are the work of the Camaldolese monk, and as we cannot logically infer that they were specially painted by him for Fra Angelico's picture, we must suppose, and indeed firmly believe them to have been added at a later time. In fact, the form of the foliated Gothic decoration lacks character and does not harmonize with the pilasters which clearly show, too, a subsequent adaptation of the frame. The finials of the pilasters do not match the style of the gables, in fact it is clear that the Gothic ornamentation, taken from some painting by Lorenzo Monaco, was at a more recent date adapted to Fra Angelico's altar-piece.

•

Fra Giovanni painted a panel picture of the "Dead Christ" for the "Compagnia del Tempio" in Florence; this is now in the Ancient and Modern Gallery, having been placed there in 1786, after the suppression of that Company. Rio supposes that the enthusiasm aroused by the great Deposition in Santa Trinità, tempted the Company to covet the possession of a similar one.[*47]

Only two figures, however, are common to the two paintings: one is the St. Simeon kneeling in the left corner who, in this second picture, is represented as a younger man than in the first; the other is a figure a little behind him, which is a reproduction of that one in the large Deposition with a hood on his head, who is speaking to the disciple below him, as he entrust to him the body of the Saviour; – a figure which Milanesi believes to be a portrait of the architect Michelozzo.

If this be indeed Fra Angelico's friend the Florentine architect, we may admit Cartier's assertion that this panel is a sequel of the larger Descent from the Cross, and may have been painted at the same time.[*48] But these are things which we dare not affirm with any certainty, as we entertain doubts regarding the greater or less authenticity of writers on the subject of Michelozzo's portrait.

Besides many figures of saints, the painter has introduced those of St. Dominic and the Beata Villana, because the Company of the Temple had ancient rights over the relics of this good woman which are preserved in the Dominican church of Santa Maria Novella. The other figures, though expressing divers feelings of sorrow and lively sympathy, have nothing in common with the famous Deposition either in character or technique and the picture does not reach the usual perfection.

Even the type of the Christ differs remarkably in the two paintings, so much so that no comparison can be instituted, or resemblance found between them; moreover, the panel of the Temple Company is badly spoilt by restoration, and the colouring is so altered that it is almost black in some parts.

•

"In the Chapel of the SS. Annunziata at Florence which Piero di Cosimo de' Medici caused to be built, Fra Angelico painted the doors of the presses where the silver plate is kept, with little figures executed with great diligence."[*49] They represent the life and death of Christ in 35 small scenes, which are now in the Ancient and Modern Gallery.

Padre Marchese writes:

"I believe it was in Fiesole that he painted many of those little panels, which may now be seen in the Gallery of the Florentine Academy of Design, and perhaps also the doors of the presses for the silver vessels in the chapel of the SS. Annunziata at Florence. In his first edition Vasari had enumerated them among his early works, which may have seemed probable, as Fra Angelico's first steps in art were in illuminating and painting small stories."[*50]

But as it was only in 1448 that Piero de' Medici, to show his devotion to the Virgin of the Annunciation, obtained from the monks the patronage of that altar with the intention of adorning it with a splendour worthy of the dignity of Her to whom it was dedicated,[*51] we cannot suppose that Fra Angelico painted the door of its treasure presses before that time.

Rio also dates at the epoch of the monk's sojourn in Tuscany towards 1450, the great unfinished painting now in the Academy of the Belle Arti, which has been regarded as one of Fra Angelico's first works. We know as a fact that in 1450 he was prior of the convent at Fiesole, and may believe that he stayed some time in Tuscany, before returning to Rome to finish the chapel of Pope Nicholas V.[*52] But Rio adds that "besides the date of the building of the chapel, the fact that the portrait of Michelozzo represents him as older in this work than in the Deposition," suggests for this cyclic composition an approximative date, very far from that assigned to it previously.[*53]

We must not forget, however, that several doubts arise as to the identity of the person representing Michelozzo.

Vasari recognises him in that old Nicodemus with a hood, who lowers the Christ from the cross in the Deposition, while Milanesi, asserting that Nicodemus has a saint's aureole not a cowl, holds that the portrait of Michelozzo is to be seen in the figure with a black hood who speaks with the disciple beneath him as he gives the body of the Lord into his hands. Certainly Milanesi has good reason to doubt Vasari's assertion, as Nicodemus has no hood: moreover Vasari himself in his second edition of the Lives (1568) assigns as the architect's likeness that very figure with a cowl who is speaking to the disciple. Therefore we must admit that the Aretian Historian was mistaken either in his indication of the figure, or in the reproduction of it as a headpiece to his Life of Michelozzo.

In any case, a similar figure to that in the "Deposition," and with the same head-gear, again appears a little older in the fresco of the convent of San Marco representing the "Adoration of the Magi"; also in another picture of the "Presentation in the Temple"; and in the little square with a "Flight into Egypt", on one of the doors of SS. Annunziata. If Michelozzo be really portrayed here, we must conclude that the Deposition was painted long before 1442, and the press doors about the same time, or a little later; but the student must take into account the curious fact that in the "Deposition" the disciple who talks to the man with a cowl above him, has also a certain resemblance to the supposed Michelozzo, and that Nicodemus reappears as St. John Baptist on the left of the large altar-piece painted for the church of San Marco, as well as in the picture of the dead Christ, and also as the kneeling King who kisses the feet of the Babe in the fresco of the "Adoration of the Magi."

Therefore, without giving great importance to the question of the true portrait of Michelozzo, we find that these heads, whether of Nicodemus or the hooded disciple, are represented in various pictures by our artist, modified by age, so that from them we may establish the succession of the different works, i.e. first the "Dead Christ" of the Company of the Temple, next the picture at San Marco (1438), then the "Deposition," and lastly the fresco in San Marco, and the little "Annunciation." Thus all these works would certainly date during Fra Angelico's stay in Florence.

•

But to return to the doors of the presses in the SS. Annunziata, it is true, as Rio writes, that instead of being a series of subjects for future frescoes or altar-pieces, the "stories" seem a hasty resumé, often too hasty, of works already painted in the convent of San Marco or other places. Some of them are noticeable for firmness of design and vigour of colouring, others instead are unworthy of the master and evidently show another hand.

To give this great work its due appreciation we must take it as a whole, as the profound genius of Fra Angelico had conceived it. Wishing to give it the unity of a dramatic poem, he placed at the beginning and at the end, like a prologue and an epilogue, two symbolic figures, in the last of which the seven branched candle-stick serves as a support to the Old and New Testaments.[*54]

We may enumerate among the best scenes the "Flight into Egypt," the "Slaughter of the Innocents," the "Betrayal of Judas," the "Dead Christ," and the "Resurrection of Lazarus," all composed in Giottesque style: but, when we think of the progress of Fra Angelico in art as shown in the frescoes in San Marco, and his best panel paintings, we cannot avoid noticing a certain want of vigour in these presses.

Having become accustomed to the grander methods of fresco painting, in which his talent and ability found greater scope for expression, – even though not attaining to the ease and force of some of his contemporaries and followers, – Fra Angelico must have now found himself at the disadvantage, natural to one who, after moving free in wider space, is suddenly cramped into narrower confines. This explains why we find in some of these small panels, greater conventionality in the representation of scenes and action, and less ease and correctness of execution. We might add also, that many of them, where these defects are especially evident, may be ascribed to other hands, less clever than his own, those of his assistants who were called in to expedite the work and assist the artist.

•

Rio believes that two of Angelico's paintings, one of which was once in the Dominican monastery of San Vincenzo d'Annalena, and the other in that of the Frati dell'Osservanza in Mugello, but now both at the Belle Arti, were executed later than the frescoes in the Vatican, to which they offer an extraordinary resemblance, not perceivable in the artist's earlier works.[*55]

We cannot, however, accept the assertion of the French critic. These two pictures, though utterly different in character and type, too forcibly recall his previous works. And as according to the same author the altar-piece of the monks of the Mugello resembles the other in colouring, technique, the freer style of drapery, the type of the Virgin and character of the figures, we might reasonably conclude that both paintings belong to the period of his residence at Fiesole or Florence, i.e. previous to his departure for Rome in 1445.

•

We are even less inclined to endorse the opinion of Rio in

regard to the date of the painting from the Annalena Convent. The internal organization of the convent was only regulated by a bull of Pope Nicholas V. after 1450, so there is probably no connection between the internal establishment of the convent and the Commission for the picture.

The convent (it is well to remember) was founded in 1453, but the religious intentions of Anna Elena Malatesta met with no slight resistance, and it was not till 1455, that Pope Calixtus III. conceded her permission to "build in her house a public oratory in which mass should be celebrated and the divine Offices performed." We cannot then admit that the picture was specially painted for the convent named[*56] after that saintly lady. When one reflects that Anna Elena Malatesta, foundress of the monastery, was educated in the house of Attilio di Vieri de' Medici, and was by Cosimo Pater Patriæ married to Baldaccio of Anghiari, it is not unlikely that the picture had been a commission from Cosimo, and that when Annalena was left a widow, and took the vows in 1441, it was offered by him to the convent, to which the sad widow had consecrated all her care. It is the more probable, that it was painted for the Medici, because the two patron saints of their house are represented in it.

SS. Cosmo and Damian only appear in the pictures painted by Fra Angelico in Florence, probably in recognition of the benefits bestowed by Cosimo on the monks of San Marco; moreover, we do not think the work could have been done at Fiesole after the first visit to Rome in 1452, because the figures, weak in chiaro-scuro, are still treated as if they were enlarged miniatures, and do not show the character of his later works. On the other hand the picture of the Osservanza in Mugello displays the whole power of the artist, and may be compared, as Rio says, to the panel at San Marco both in the character of the figures and the larger style of treatment.

Vasari cites other works which have unfortunately been dispersed or destroyed, among which were an altar-piece in the Certosa at Florence, representing the "Virgin and Child," with some angels below, and at the sides St. Laurence, St. Zenobi, and St. Benedict; the "Coronation of the Madonna," once in the lunette of the Acciajoli chapel: another with the "Virgin and two saints," painted "con azzurri oltramarini bellissimi," (with beautiful ultramarine blues): and the pictures in the dividing wall of Santa Maria Novella opposite the choir. The "Annunciation," which according to Vasari was in the church of San Francesco at San Miniato, and which Milanesi believes to be in the Museum of Madrid, is instead now in the National Gallery at London. It is a diptych, in one panel the archangel Gabriel, with golden wings outspread, crossing his hands on his breast bows before the Virgin, who in the other panel leans forward to listen to his blessed word. The scene is in a cloister, from the arches of which a field of flowers is seen, and in the distant horizon the outlines of the Apennine mountains. A great lily blossoms beside the Virgin, the two capitals of the columns of the cloister have the Albizzi arms carved on them.

"This good Father painted so many pictures for the houses of the citizens of Florence, that one wonders how one man could so perfectly execute even in many years all that he has done." So writes Vasari, and indeed a complete list of his paintings still existing in Italy and elsewhere would be too long; those we have illustrated will, however, suffice to give a good idea of his artistic genius, and the sentiment with which this gentle artist could represent the marvellous visions of a soul in love with heaven!

IV

FRA ANGELICO

AT ROME AND ORVIETO

[1445-1455.]

These many and various labours – writes Vasari –

"having rendered the name of Fra Giovanni illustrious throughout all Italy, he was invited to Rome by Pope Nicholas V., who caused him to adorn the chapel of the palace, where the pontiff is accustomed to hear mass, with a "Deposition from the Cross," and with certain events from the life of San Lorenzo, which are admirable."[*57]

But Vasari errs in giving to Nicholas V. the merit of having called Fra Angelico to Rome; he is also mistaken in affirming that the artist was offered the archbishopric of Florence, and on his modest refusal Sant' Antonino was proposed to the Pope: "and because Fra Giovanni appearing to the Pope to be, as he really was, a person of most holy life, gentle and modest, the archbishopric of Florence having then become vacant, he judged him worthy of that preferment."[*58]

It was instead Pope Eugene IV., who wishing to embellish the Vatican with pictures, invited Fra Angelico to Rome in 1445, having admired his sanctity of life, and talent in art when in Florence. That Pope died the following year, but in his successor Nicholas V., Fra Angelico found another sincere admirer and friend, and he remained in Rome to finish the works he had begun. He painted two chapels in the Vatican, the one of the Sacrament for Eugene IV., the other for Pope Nicholas V., whose name it still bears. The former was pulled down by Pope Paul III. to improve the staircase.

> "In this work," says Vasari, "which was an excellent one, Fra Giovanni had in his own admirable manner painted stories in fresco from the life of Christ, and had introduced many portraits of eminent persons then living. These portraits would most probably have been lost to us, had not Paulo Jovius caused the following among them to be preserved for his Museum: Pope Nicholas V., the Emperor Frederick, who had at that time arrived in Italy; Fra Antonino, who afterwards became Archbishop of Florence; Biondo da Forlì, and Ferdinand of Arragon."[*59]
> •

It is probable that after having finished the chapel of the Sacrament, and before the new commission was given by Nicholas V., Fra Angelico – by means of Don Francesco di Barone of Perugia, a Benedictine monk and celebrated master of glass painting – entered into negotiation with the Operai and Consuls of the Duomo at Orvieto, to paint the chapel of the Madonna di San Brizio. But before he accepted the commission he gave them to understand that he could only go to Orvieto in the months of June, July and August, when he did not wish to remain in Rome.

> "He demanded 200 gold ducats a year, together with all expenses of board and lodging, colours and scaffolding; besides seven ducats a month for his assistant, and two for his boy. The contract was signed on these conditions by Messer Enrico Monaldeschi, the principal citizen – almost the tyrant – of Orvieto, who always took a personal part in the most important events of the city. Fra Angelico took with

him Benozzo di Lese, Giovanni di Antonio da Firenze, and Iacomo di Poli, with whose assistance he commenced the painting in the large lunettes on June 15th 1447. Pietro di Niccola of Orvieto was also employed. They painted together for three months and a half, but Fra Angelico did not return the following year.

"As the summer of 1449 drew near, the overseers, who were left with only Pietro Baroni, a proved artist, endeavoured to persuade Fra Angelico to go back again, and join Baroni, saying that if he failed them, they would prefer to postpone the work, as they looked more to the beauty than the expense, as they always had been accustomed to do. When every hope of obtaining Fra Angelico was lost, they gave Benozzo Gozzoli a trial to continue Fra Giovanni's frescoes,"[*60] but the effect was not happy.

Fra Angelico painted in the roof of the chapel a "Christ in Judgment," surrounded by a "glory" of angels. Sixteen saints and prophets are seated on clouds with the motto: *Prophetarum laudabilis numerus*. The Saviour in a circle of light raises His right hand on high, while the left supports a globe on His knees. On both sides are groups of angels in varied attitudes of adoration. The prophets stand out in pyramidal groups on a background of gold, and are either reading or meditating with religious calm. Rosini judges the Christ to be the work of Benozzo Gozzoli, because it seems inferior to the prophets, which show a grander treatment and better execution.

"I think," he writes, "that the prophets alone belong to Fra Angelico; the Christ in glory, and the remainder to Benozzo and the others. I am led to this not only by their different style, but the heads of the prophets, although they are disposed one above the other, as the space demands, show the more dignified style, and perfect execution of the Florentine monk. That perfection ought to be seen also in the Christ, which seems to me to be a little inferior to them."[*61]

But even while admitting that the features of the Saviour have in some parts the characteristics of Benozzo's style, we must not forget that he derived from his master both his good and bad points, and from the latter especially originated those peculiar defects, which are greatly emphasized in Benozzo's works. Hence it is natural that something of the scholar's manner should appear in that face, but it is no proof that he has worked at it. On the contrary it is enough to prove the impossibility of ascribing this figure to him, to glance at the head of Christ in Benozzo's fresco in the church of St. Francis at Montefalco, representing the meeting of St. Francis and St. Dominic. High up on the left the Saviour raises His right hand and the Virgin kneels at His feet. Now all the figures are absolutely wanting in dignity and character, especially the downcast head of Christ, with its projecting forehead and receding chin, which is absolutely vulgar. Here Benozzo has not even distantly remembered any of his master's noble representations of the Saviour. Therefore not only had he no part in that figure at Orvieto, but neither could he have done the prophets, for they are far superior to the Christ. Finally, it is not probable that Fra Angelico, with the feeling which inspired his work, should entrust to an assistant the execution of such an important figure as the Christ.

Even though the figure of the Christ is not to be compared to the finest of the prophets, yet we find in the countenance the same characteristics as the other heads display. True, it looks worse than it really is, for a crack in the roof has damaged the mouth and beard, and the fresco has besides suffered in the restorer's hands.

It is a known fact, that a few months after Fra Angelico left, it was necessary to repair the roof of the chapel in which he had worked, on account of the rain that percolated there, to the great detriment of the paintings.

However this may be, it is certain that the heads of the prophets have sweetness of expression and nobility of character, and all the figures are remarkable for their fine form, dignified attitudes, free and simple draperies, combined with bright and vivid colouring. These qualities are not so visible in the compartment of our Lord and the adoring angels, which may with more certainty be attributed to Benozzo.

•

Fra Angelico returned to Rome on the 28th of September in

that year (1447) and never went back to Orvieto, but his reasons for breaking his contract and leaving a work incomplete are not explained. Perhaps he perceived the difficulties of the composition and was arrested by the terrifying dread – which his character and feeling would have magnified – of painting a Last Judgment in such grand proportions. Or he may have had an intuition, that his work would never be worthy of that famous building, especially as he was called on to depict the punishments of hell and the various feelings of sorrow, passion and despair in the damned souls, sentiments so foreign to his own nature. Or possibly the desire to finish the paintings entrusted to him in Rome by the new Pontiff Nicholas V., induced him to break his contract. In the absence of more precise records it is difficult to establish the truth.

Certain it is that Fra Angelico left Orvieto for Rome and that he painted there a "Studio" or Chapel for Nicholas V., for which the payment is entered in a register dated 1449, but "after this year," writes Müntz, "we find no more traces of the illustrious Dominican, in the books of the secret treasury."[*62]

On January 10th 1452 Fra Angelico is again at Fiesole as prior of his convent, and in the same year the rulers of the Commune of Prato employed the good offices of Archbishop Antonino to induce Fra Angelico to paint the principal chapel of their church; but he refused, and the commission was given to Filippo Lippi.

•

The fact that the name of the Dominican artist has not been found in the registers of the Vatican Treasury after 1449, need not necessarily be taken as a proof that he was not working in the Chapel of Nicholas V. at a later date. Indeed, as he went no more to Orvieto, and would not undertake to paint the Choir of the Prato Cathedral, it seems probable that he should have gone back to Rome to finish his work there. The chapel which preserves these precious frescoes by Angelico may be considered one of the most famous monuments of Italian art.

On three of the walls, he has represented in two lines of

frescoes the Vocation, the Apostleship, and the Martyrdom of St. Stephen and St. Laurence. On the first side St. Stephen receives the Communion from St. Peter, and distributes alms to the poor: on the second are his preaching and justification before the high priest: in the third his lapidation. Below on the first wall is the consecration of St. Laurence, and his almsgiving to the poor and maimed; second, his imprisonment and the conversion of the jailer; and lastly his martyrdom.

The design is free and firm, yet keeping true to the character of the artist. The execution is more accurate and equal; although less realistic than that of Masaccio, yet he succeeds in giving his figures a greater grace and softer expression, indeed, the sentiment with which he imbues his figures, was never reached by any other artist, and that sentiment is here more admirably expressed than in any other of his works.

Whether St. Stephen be kneeling in wrapt devotion to take the chalice, or with the love of divine charity giving money to the woman, while the little child gives him its hand; whether touching his thumb he seems to explain some religious question, while some women seated there hang on his words, exchange their impressions, or ecstatically clasp their hands in sign of admiration or faith; whether he speak before the Great Council, or is conducted at last torture, supporting it with faith and resignation; – his noble figure always inspires a feeling of profound piety, of serene calm and personal devotion.

Although the representation of buildings is still too fantastic, the perspective is not neglected as in some other works. In the "Ordination of St. Stephen," the design of the interior of the church is in good architectural style, but the canopy above the altar is so low in proportion to the figure of St. Peter, that if he were to rise to his full height he could not stand at the altar; in another the open space in which St. Stephen is preaching has a fortress on the right, and a palace of very doubtful character in the background.

The details of ornamentation, however, are very carefully

designed, the motives of the decoration being refined and elegant. The pilasters with their pretty candelabra and capitals rich with sculpture, combine so harmoniously with the purer architectural forms, as to produce a most pleasing effect and show the result of his studies among the numberless remains of ancient Rome.

•

The St. Laurence series is not less beautiful. It is marvellous that Fra Angelico could express motives so analogous to the former set of frescoes without repeating himself. Sixtus II., drawn with the lineaments of Nicholas V., consecrates to the diaconal office St. Laurence, who reverently kneeling extends both hands to receive the sacramental cup. Around them are some fine figures of ecclesiastics, who, robed in magnificent vestments, assist at the ceremony, together with deacons and acolytes, who hold the book and censer. There is, it is true, a great sameness in the heads, which suggests that most of them were studied from the same model.

In another fresco, the Pope consigns the treasures of the church to the saint, while a monk turns brusquely round at the noise made at the door by two soldiers who come to conduct St. Laurence to martyrdom. But where Fra Angelico has best succeeded in fully rendering his sentiment, is in the painting which represents the distribution of alms.

Angelico evidently delights in the thought of the inner satisfaction of the saint, and the happiness of the recipients; and the sincere and serene joy transfused in the countenances of the different figures is expressed with unusual ability and extraordinary truth to nature.

He has enlivened the severity of the scene by the episode of two children, who are laughingly struggling over a piece of money received. Infantile grace and content breathe in their features, though slightly disturbed by the doubt which of them will remain possessor of the precious gift.

The two last frescoes are very attractive and equally

admirable. One represents the condemnation of St. Laurence, the other his martyrdom. The study of classic art is still more manifest in these than in the others, for not only the architecture, but even the niches which contain statues are imitated from the antique. In the "Condemnation" the Emperor Decius wears a cuirass with a toga over it fastened on the right shoulder, as in the ancient imperial busts. His sceptre is terminated by a little idol, and above his throne is the Roman eagle with outspread wings, in a garland of bay leaves: in the other fresco the statues appear to be reproductions of ancient Roman monuments. But unfortunately this last picture has been so injured and restored that we cannot fully appreciate its value.

The execution of these pictures is really remarkable. Fra Angelico, as we have said, without losing his fundamental qualities, has acquired and here reveals new qualities; the four Evangelists among the clouds on a background of blue, dotted with golden stars, are noble and full of character; the figures of the saints on the simulated pilasters, and at the corners of each side of the chapel, might be classed among Fra Angelico's best. Who does not remember above the rest the fine and noble figure of St. Bonaventure, with his flowing white beard, thoughtful eyes, and an aspect of goodness and seriousness combined that is quite enchanting? What other figure, however beautiful, can show such just proportions, solid form, and majestic design, such a strong character and expression as this? The saint's thoughtful gaze is turned to the left, his mouth lightly indicating a smile, or rather the sweet expression of innate goodness, the marvellously drawn hands support an open book which rests on his side. Here Fra Angelico reveals his skill in all its fulness; and when we reflect on his advanced age, we can only remain in admiring surprise before the freshness of his creative power, and the force of his execution.

•

We have documental evidence that Benozzo Gozzoli assisted his master in these frescoes, and doubtless we may attribute to him the fine decorations, where roses bud amidst flowers and foliage of every kind, and garlands are resting on pretty little children's heads, or are festooned on medallions bearing the tiara, and crossed keys of Nicholas V.; but we cannot give him the merit of having beautified the scenes of the "Preaching of St. Stephen," or "St. Laurence distributing alms."[*63]

We admit the probability that Benozzo may have executed some of the figures, but there is a difference between this and supposing that he had any conspicuous part in the compositions, especially in the St. Laurence series, which we cannot believe. If the whole scene were indeed by Benozzo, would not the difference of hand between master and scholar be more strikingly evident? And the more so, as the scholar had not yet reached mastery of technique, and his early frescoes show a certain crudeness, want of harmony and incorrectness of design, which far remove them from the proved technical ability of his master. Nor can we believe that he timidly followed the lines traced on the walls by Fra Angelico, for even in that case something peculiar to himself must have been clearly perceptible in them. Now this, to speak frankly, is not evident.

None of the women assisting at the preaching of St. Stephen recall the characteristic type of those which Benozzo painted in the frescoes at Montefalco. The saint's listeners have regular features, and remind one of the various female figures in the San Marco frescoes ("Resurrection of Christ" and "Prayer on the Mount of Olives"). Benozzo's handling is less solid, his outlines are hard and sharp, colouring crude and chiaroscuro weak; in the stories of St. Laurence we find instead, and in a very high degree, the solidity and correctness which we have admired in Fra Angelico's Florentine paintings. It suffices to recall the "Adoration of the Magi," in San Marco, one of his last works before leaving for Rome, and the beautiful prophets at Orvieto; in both these pictures we meet with the same types and figures as in the Roman frescoes, especially in those representing "St. Peter ordaining St. Stephen," "St. Laurence distributing alms," and "St.

Stephen before the high priest." Without then following up doubtful suppositions, it does not seem admissible that Fra Angelico, old as he was, should have ceded to his pupil either the direction, or the greater part of works of such importance, which it was greatly to his interest to finish with the utmost care and perfection.

Cavalcaselle remarks that the severity of the Orvietans who would not let Benozzo finish the work which Fra Angelico had left incomplete, is inexplicable; but we must remember that though Benozzo imitated his master's style, the inferiority of his talent was always apparent in the common types, false anatomy, and mistaken proportions of his figures. "He does not equal the master who guided him in his first years, but he follows his style as much as he can, with less talent." [*64]

It was not therefore Benozzo's work which enlarged the master's style, but in the Vatican frescoes the master clearly shows the effort he has himself made to render the action of his figures more grand, his painting more solid, figures more characteristic and the episodes with which his admirable compositions are enriched more fundamentally truthful.

These paintings prove that he had reached his greatest artistic development; although always retaining his innate character he concedes to the new requirements of art as much of his temperament and sentiment, as he can conscientiously yield. Thus his works display a continuous improvement, each new stage in the long road of his artistic career, represents a fresh conquest, a new and remarkable progress. His pupils and collaborators limited themselves to aiding him, and rendering his work lighter in parts of secondary importance, but he needed no other help to be, and always remain, worthy of the high company in which he finds himself in the Vatican.

•

In the Sixtine Chapel, near the quiet creations of the artists of the Renaissance, the power and awful force of Michelangelo stand out; in the "Stanze" Raphael has left an everlasting wealth of artistic treasures; and in the Chapel of Nicholas V. Fra Angelico with ingenuous expression and the purest and most sincere religious feeling, painted his master-piece.

But notwithstanding the great difference between the former giants of art, and our saintly artist, he is quite worthy of their glorious company.

The sweet gentleness of his character was all that hindered him from a more exact and deep study of reality, but it was precisely by means of this character that he succeeded, as no one else could do, in expressing the elevated ideas of his serene and calm soul, profound inspiration and naïve freshness of faith.

In 1455 after a life entirely dedicated to art, Fra Giovanni, at the age of 68 years, died in Rome, having well earned the grateful veneration of posterity. The austere virtues of his soul gained him the title of *Beato* (blessed) and for the lovely lines traced by his brush, he was called *Angelico*. A marble monument was erected over his tomb in the church of the Minerva, with his effigy and the following inscription, said to have been dictated by Pope Nicholas V. himself:

HIC JACET VEN. PICTOR
FR. JO. DE FLOR. ORD. P.
M
CCCC
L
V

Non mihi sit laudi, quod eram velut alter Apelles,
Sed quod lucra tuis omnia, Christe, dabam;
Altera nam terris opera extant, altera cœlo;
Urbs me Joannem Flos tulit Etruriæ.

"Give me not praise for being almost a second Apelles, but because I gave to thy poor, O Christ, all my earnings. Thus part of my work remains on earth and part in heaven. My home was in that city, which is the Flower of Etruria."

Illustrations of art by contemporaries of Fra Angelico on the following pages.

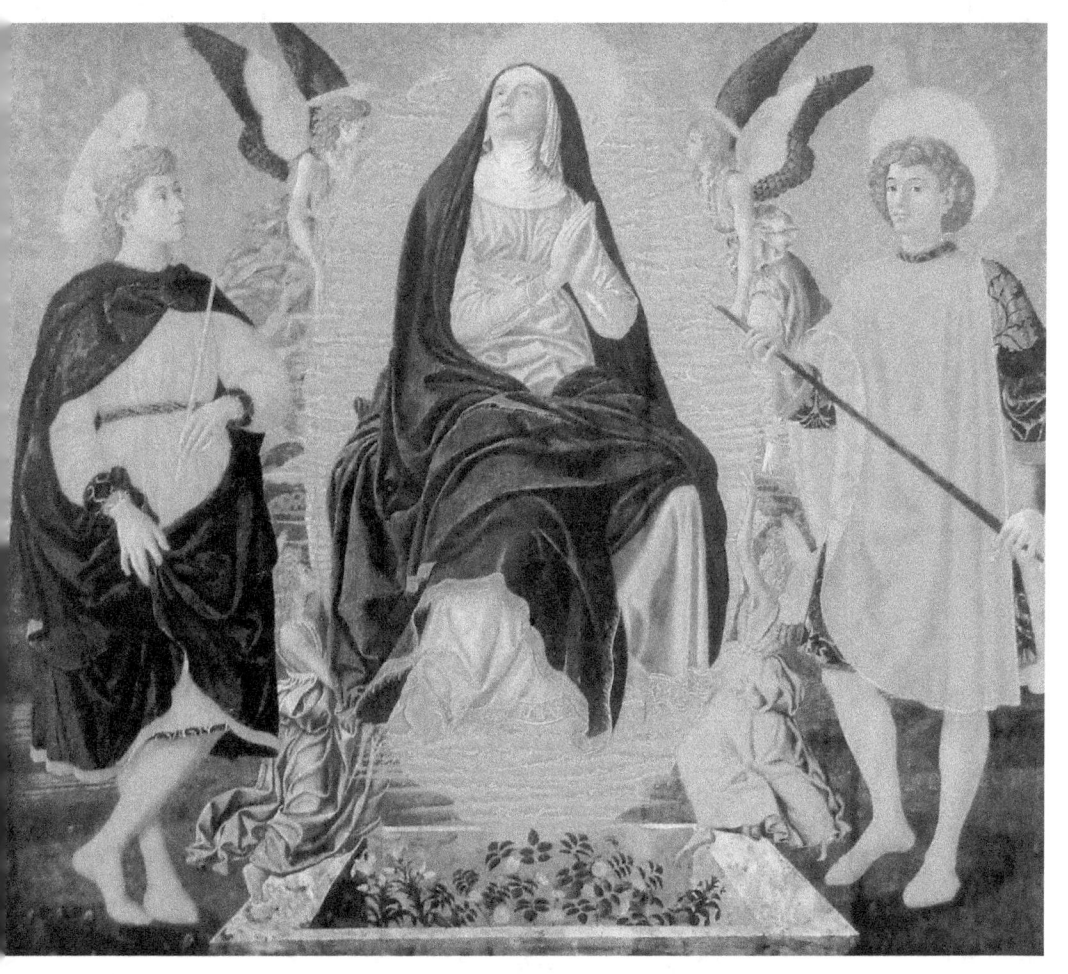

Andrea del Castagno, Assumption, Berlin

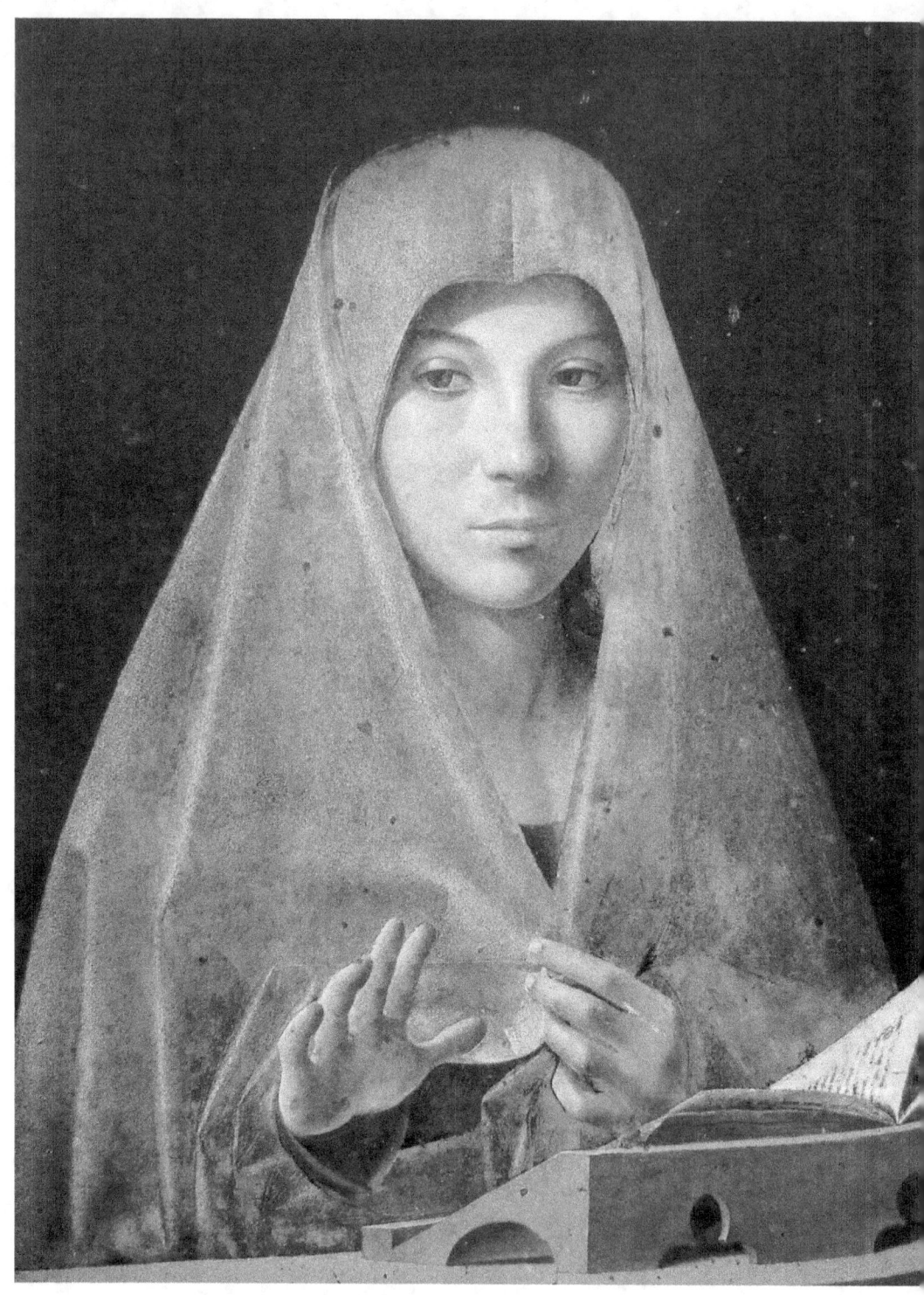

Antonello da Messina, The Virgin of the Annunciation, 1475, Palermo

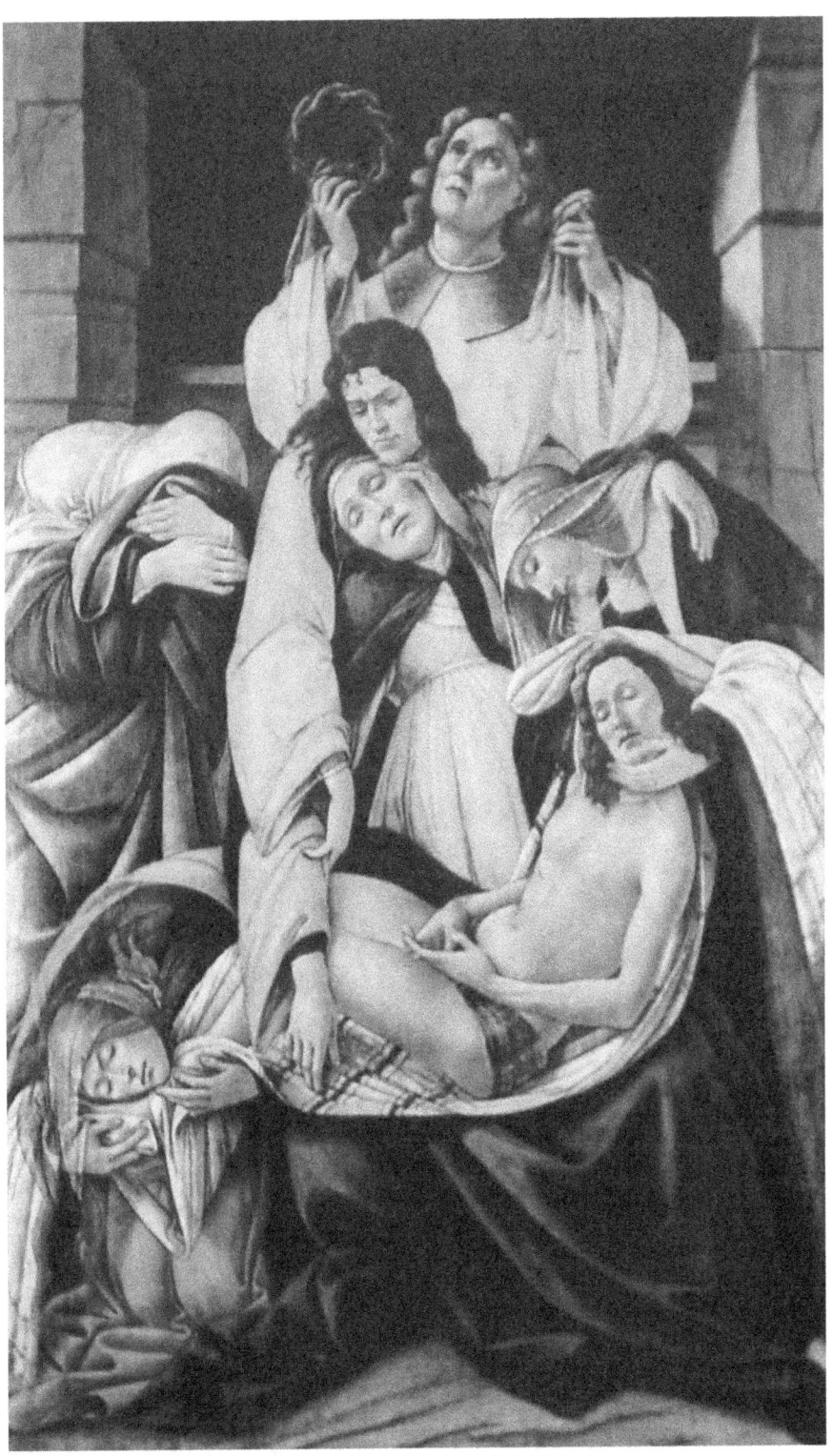

Sandro Botticelli, *Pietà*, Museo Poldi Pezzoli, Milan

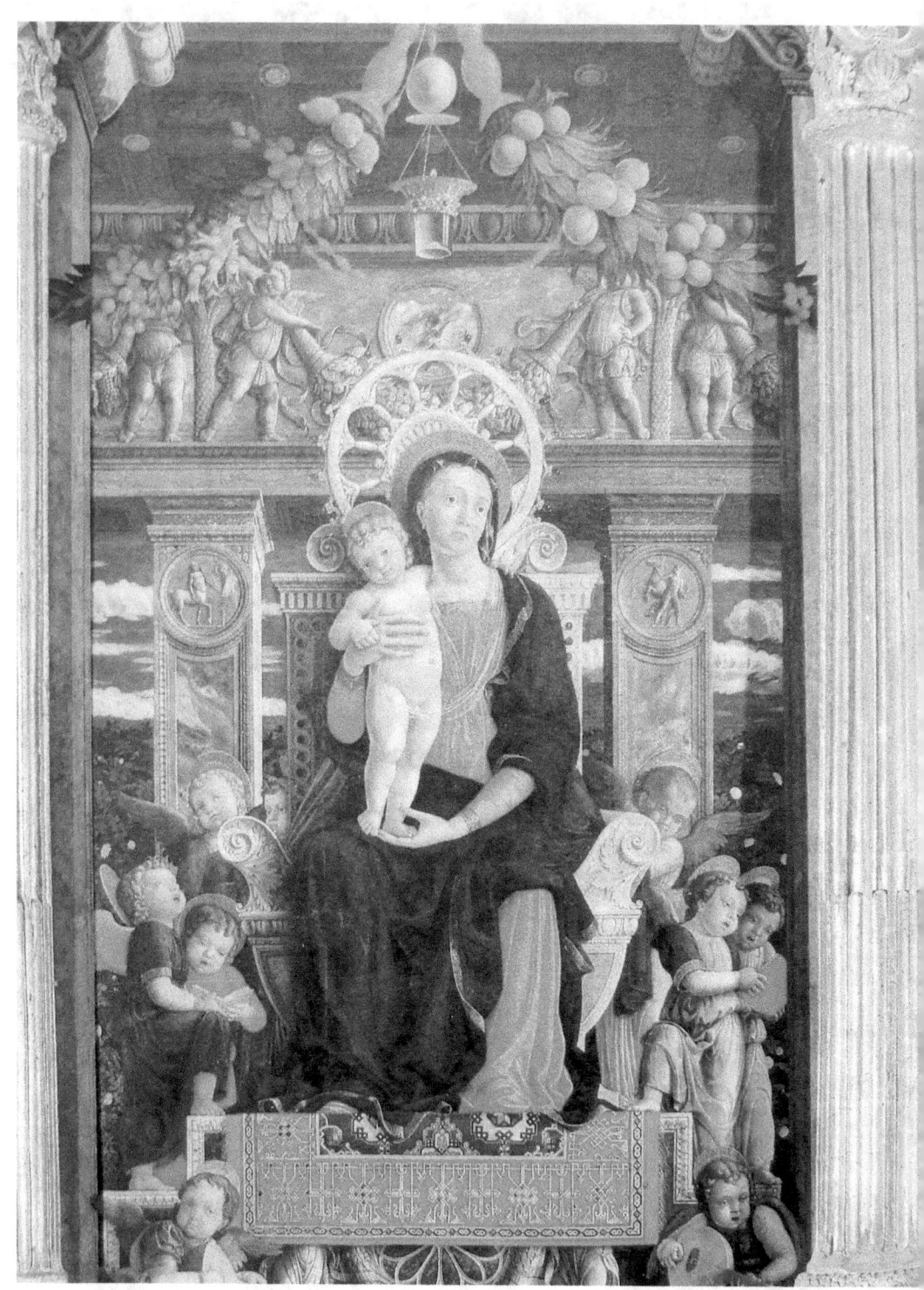

Andreas Mantegna, Madonna and Child Enthroned, 1457-60, Verona

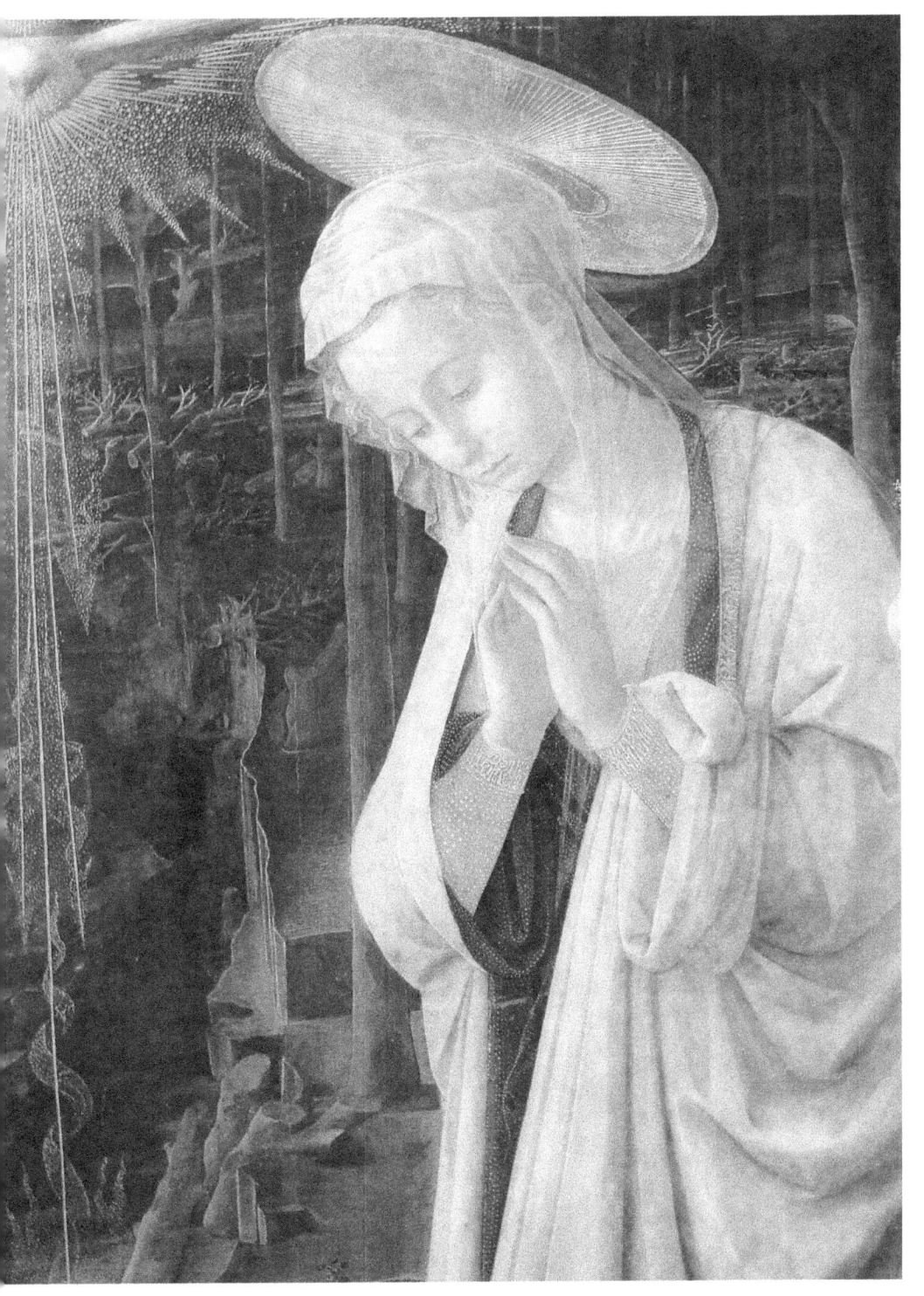

Fra Filippo Lippi, The Adoration of the Virgin, Berlin, detail

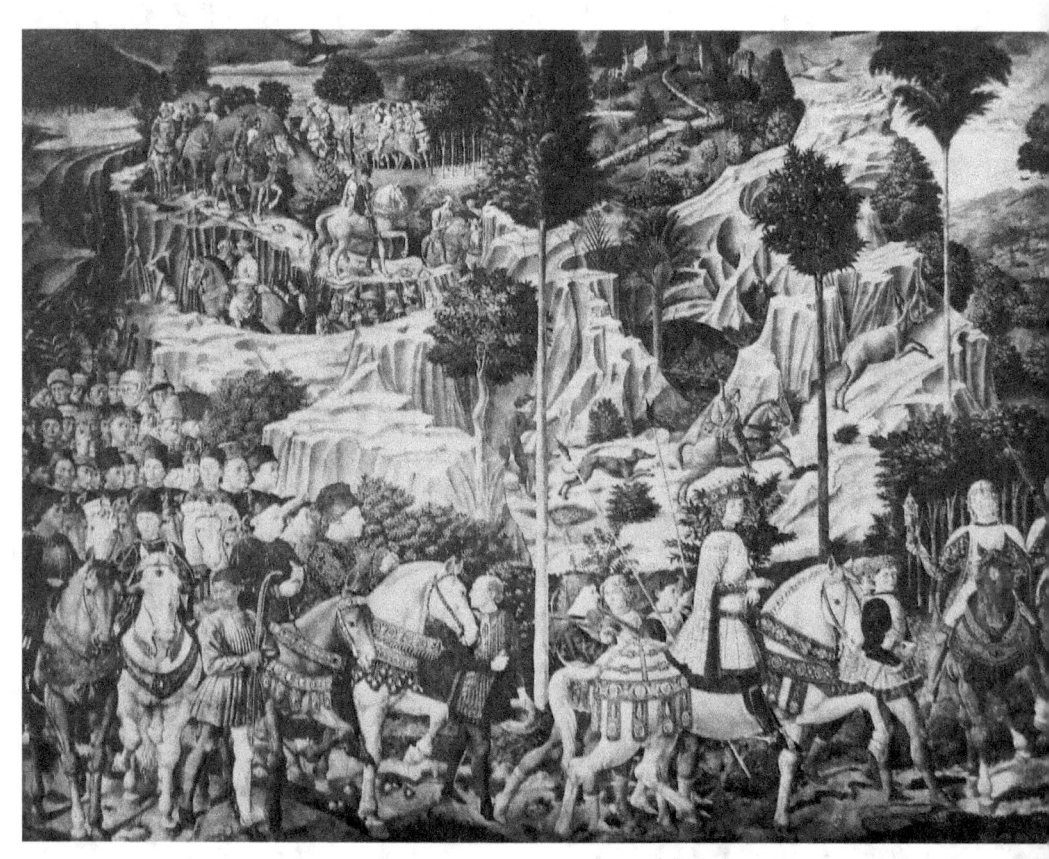

Benozzo Gozzoli, Journey of the Magi

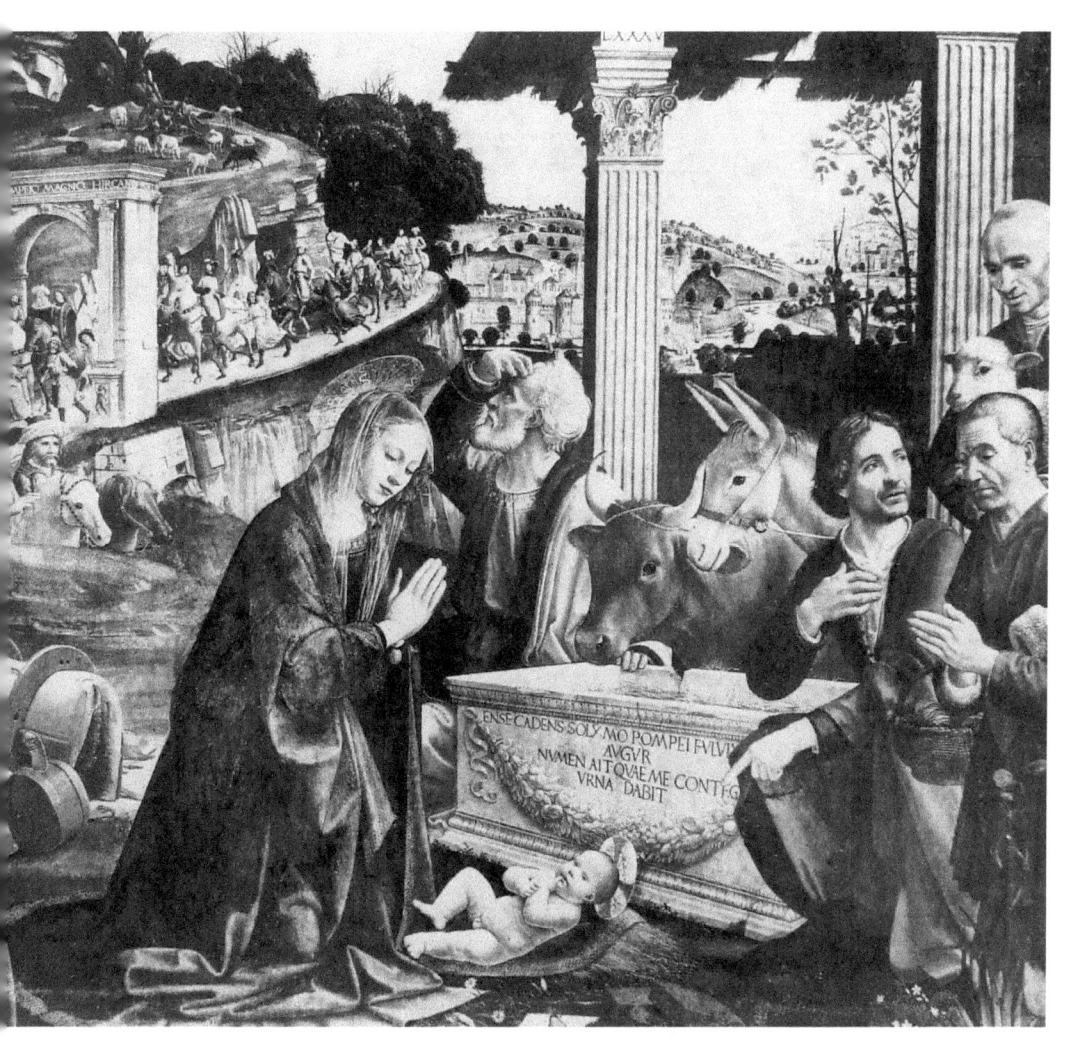

Domenico Ghirlandaio, Adoration of the Shepherds, 1485

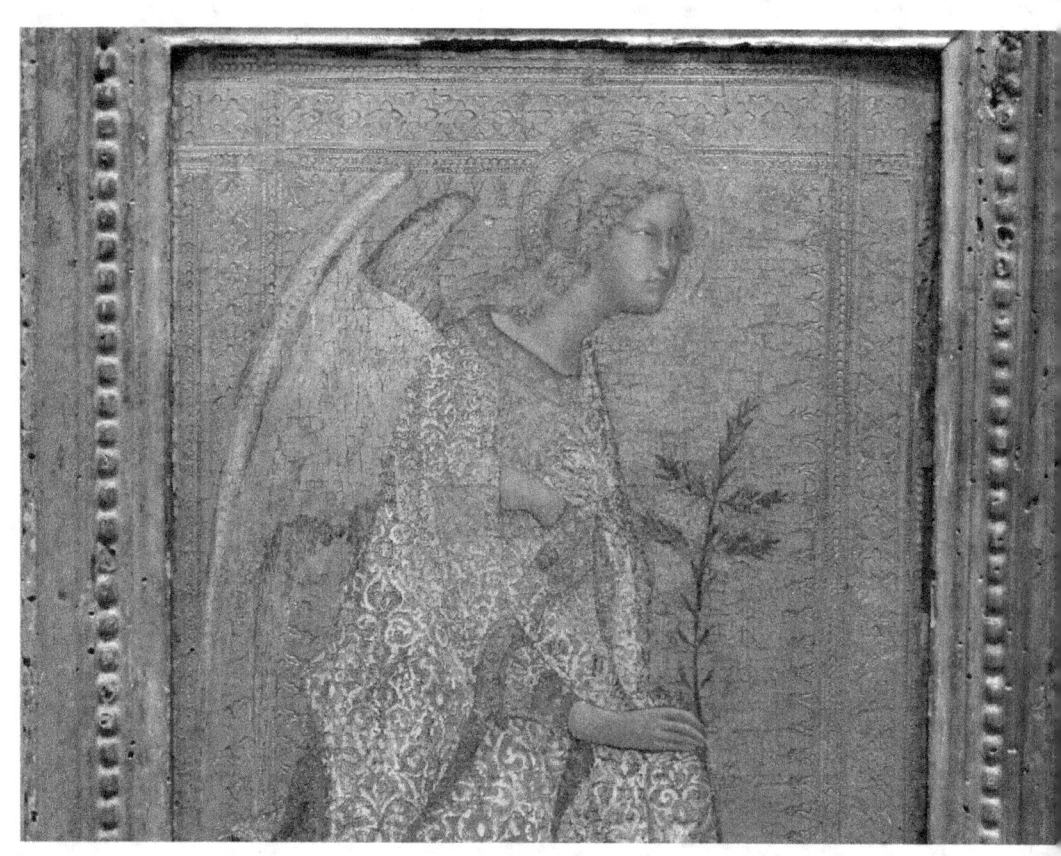

Simone Martini, Annunciation, Metropolitan Museum of Art, New York

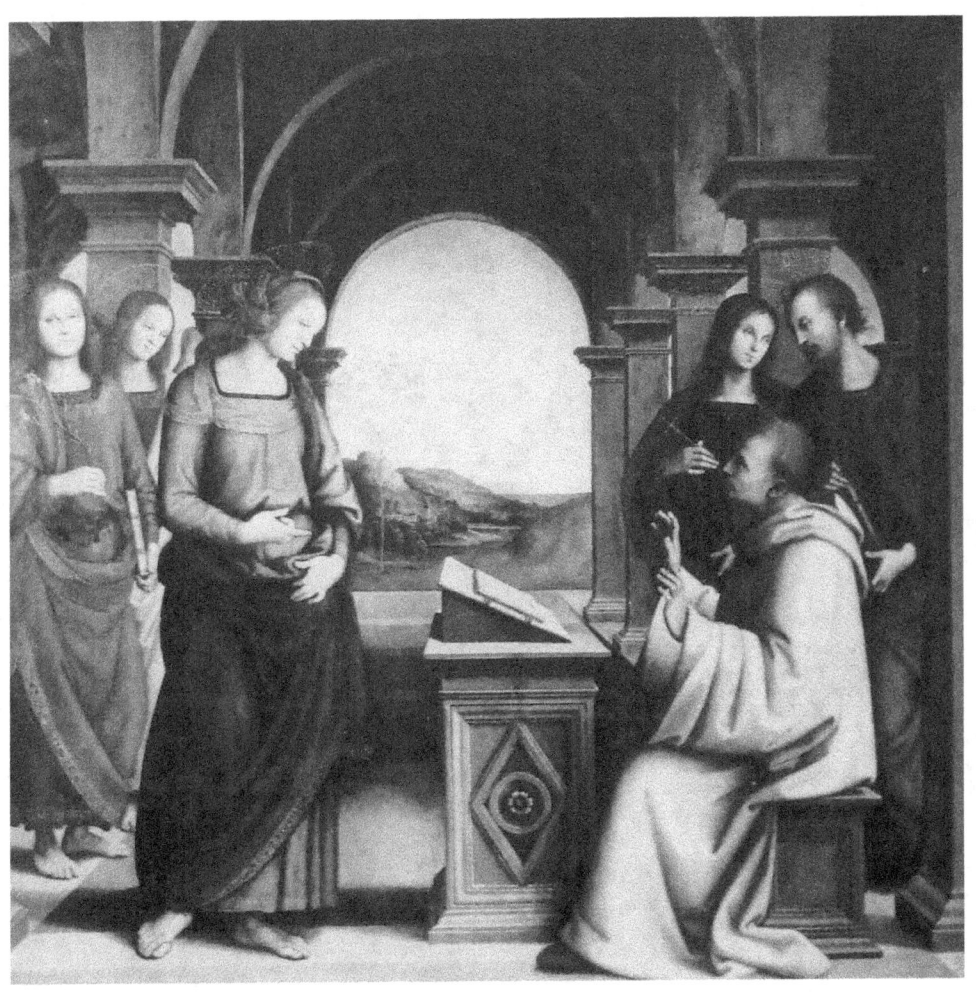

Perugino, Vision of St Bernard, 1488

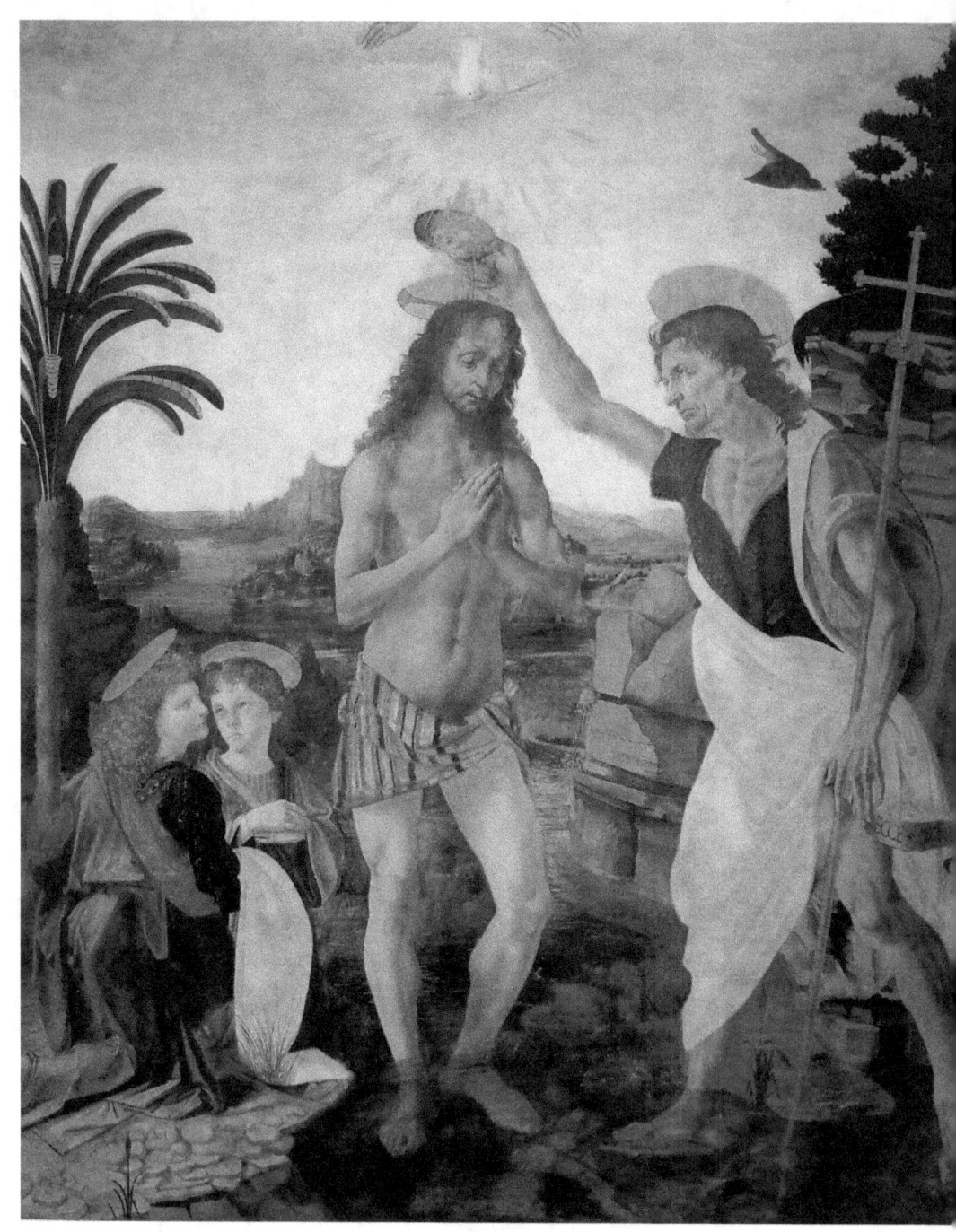

Andrea del Verrocchio, The Baptism of Christ

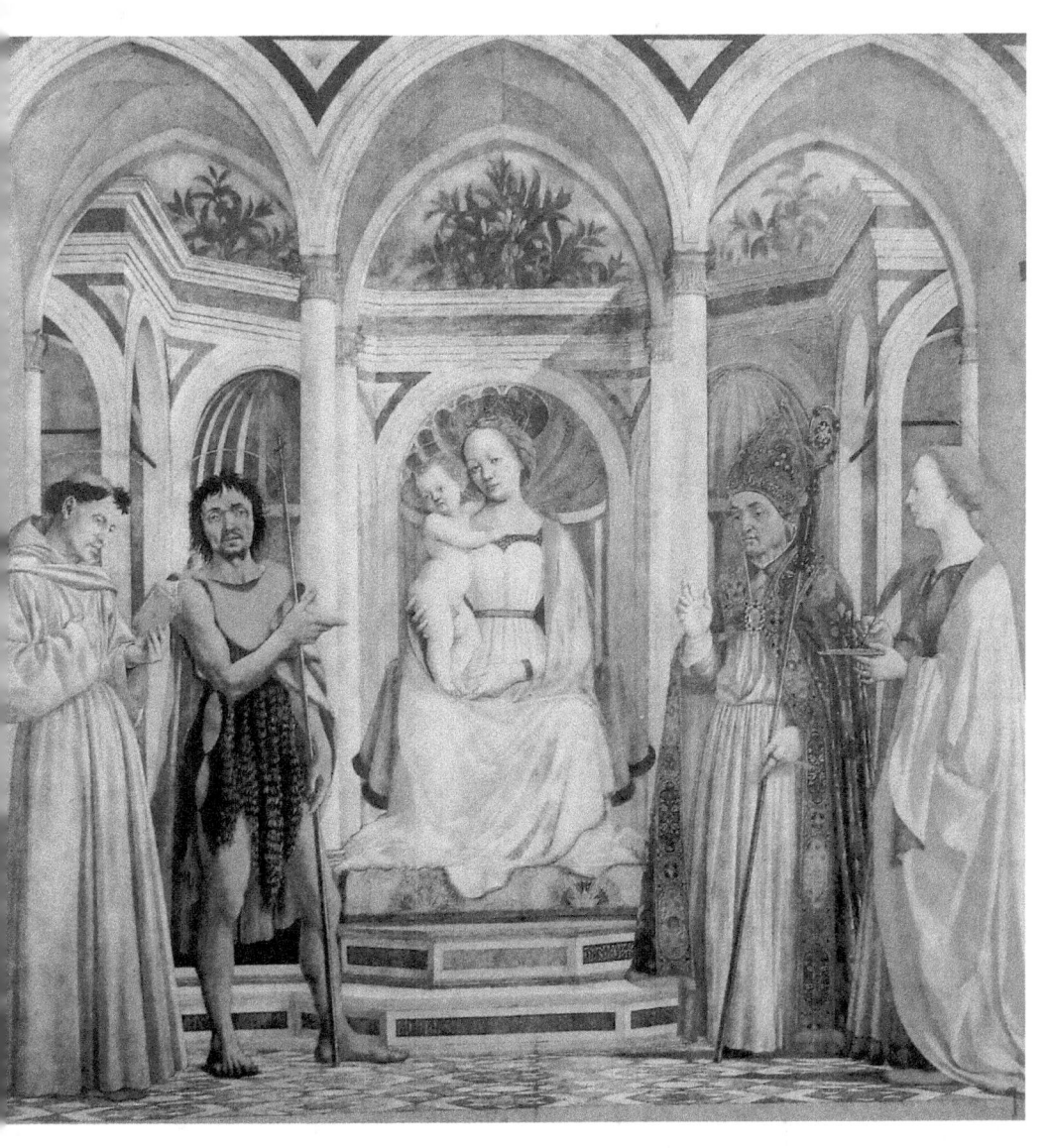

Domenico Veneziano, Madonna and Child With Saints, 1445, Uffizi Gallery

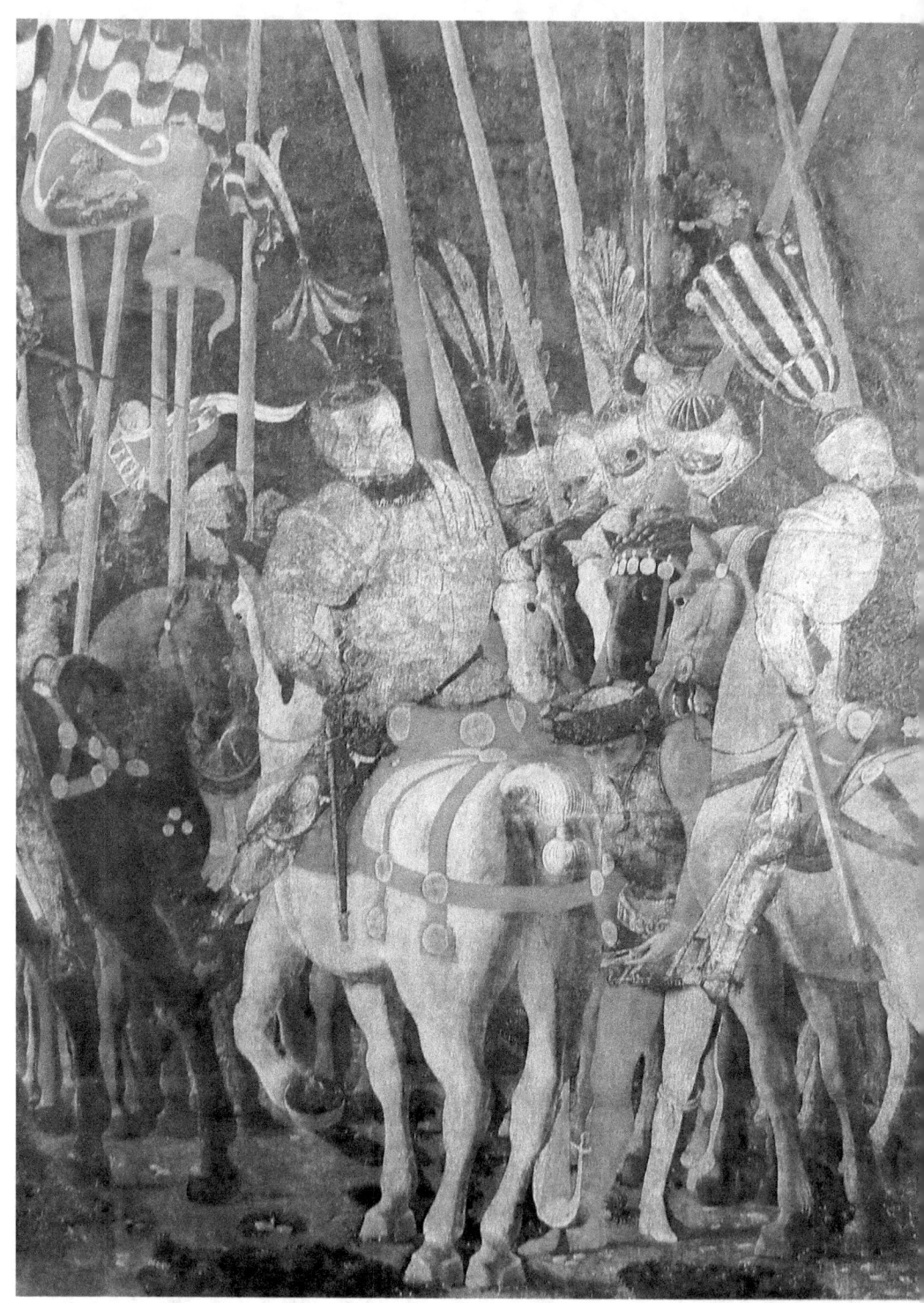

Paolo Uccello, Battle of San Romano, 1456-60, Loure, Paris

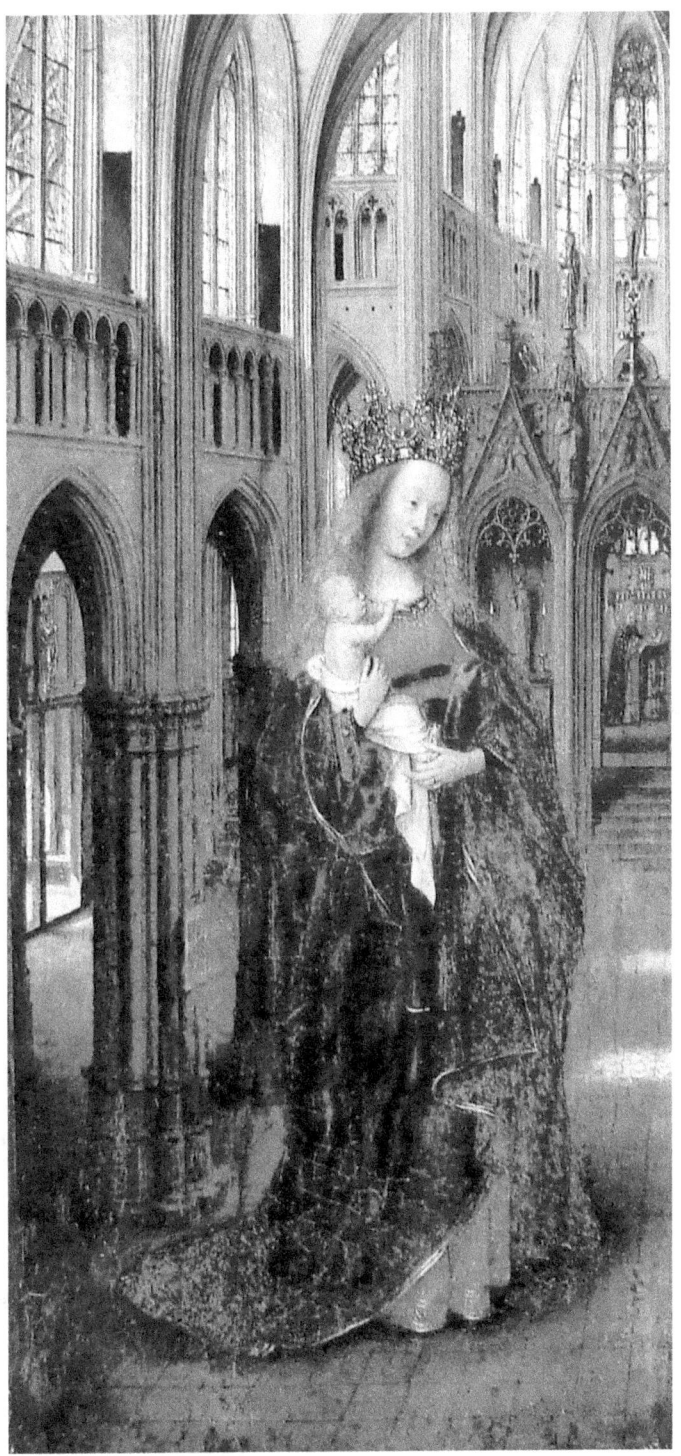

Jan van Eyck, Madonna In a Church, Berlin

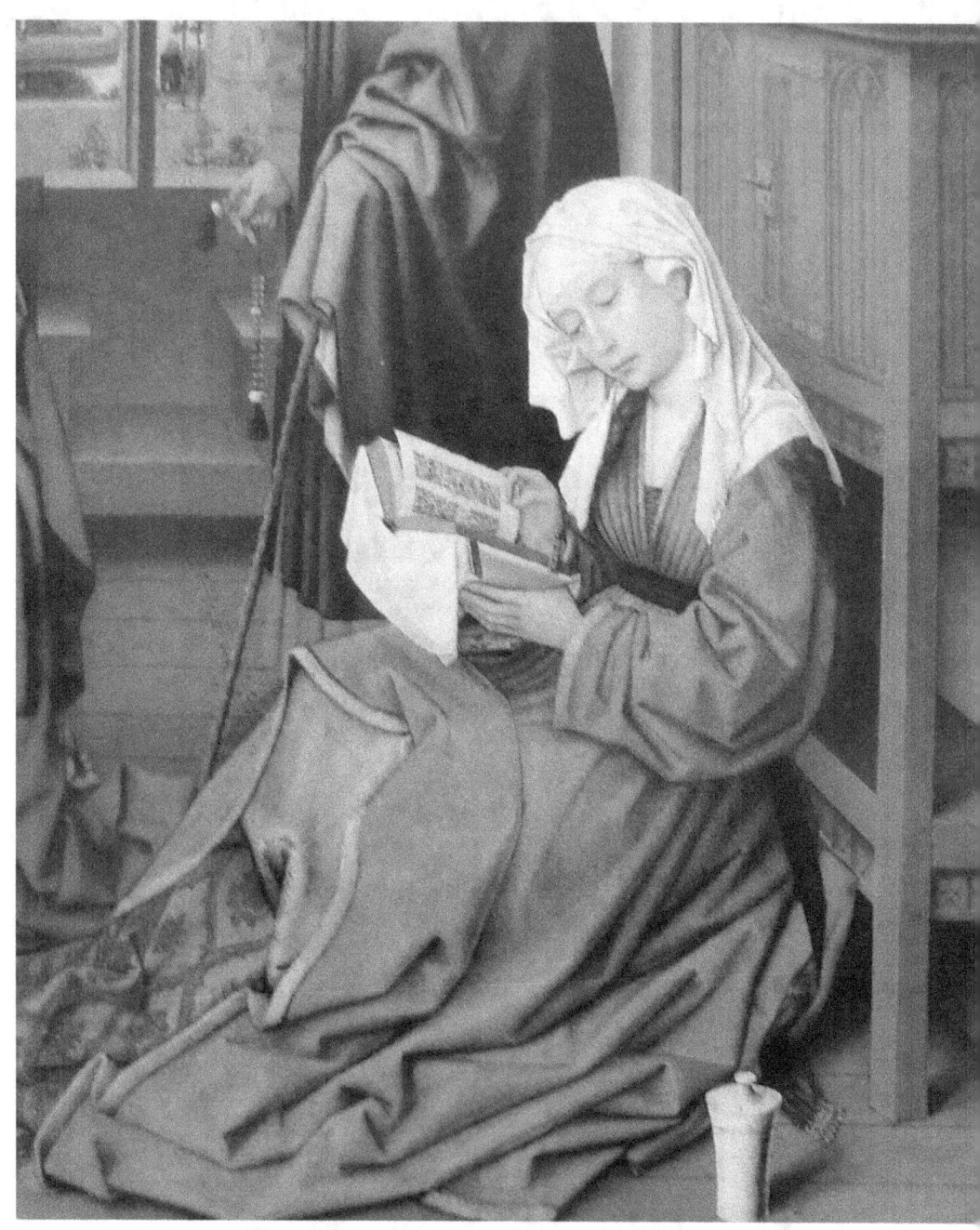

Rogier van der Weyden, Mary Magdalene Reading, detail, National Gallery, London

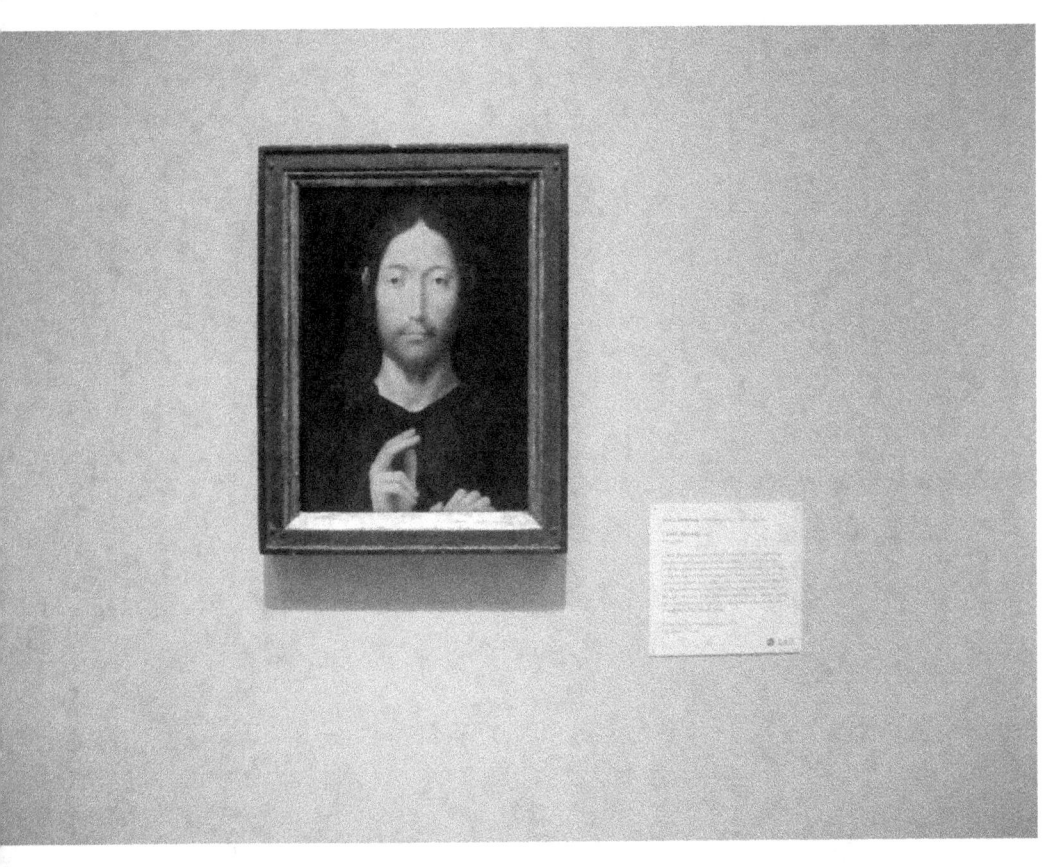

Hans Memling, Christ Blessing, Metropolitan Museum of Art

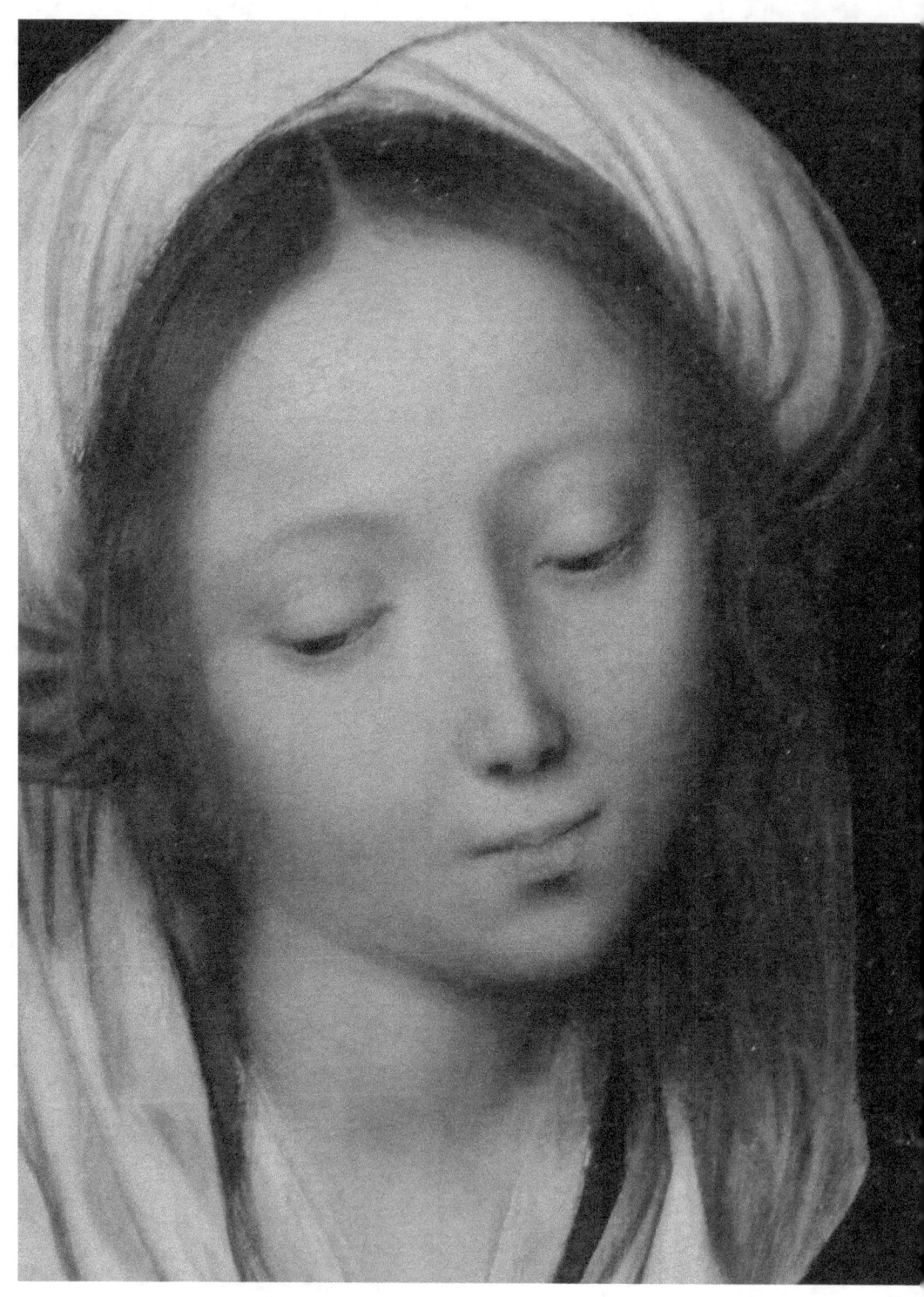

Gerard David, detail of the Adoration, Metropolitan Museum of Art

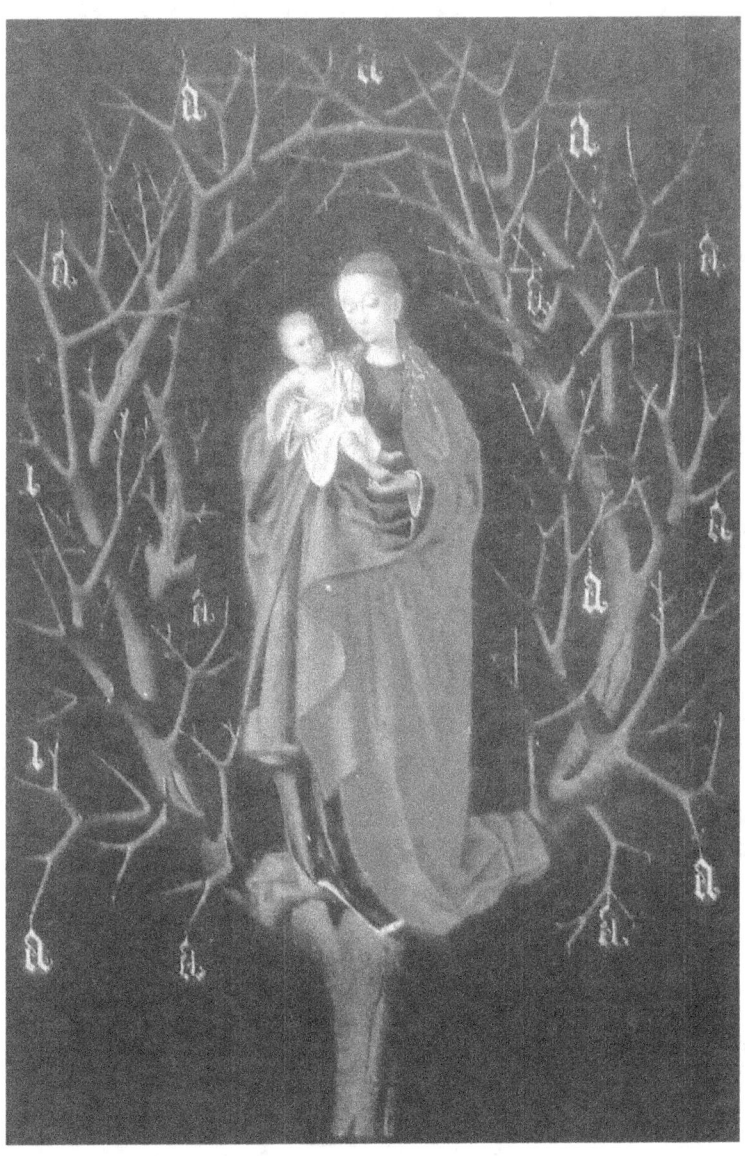

Petrus Christus, Madonna In a Barren Tree, 1450,
Prado, Madrid

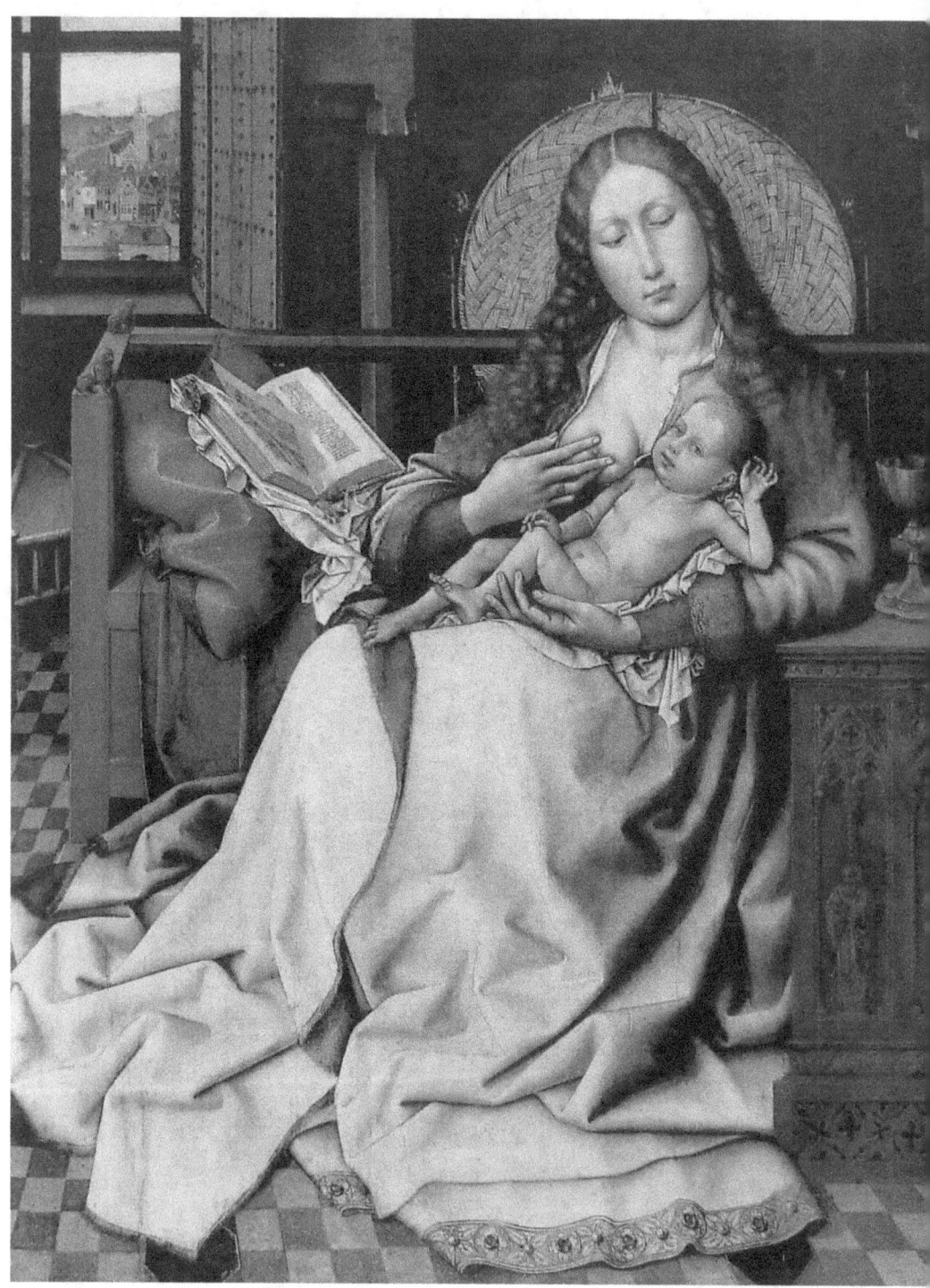

Robert Campin, Madonna With the Firescreen, National Gallery, London

FOOTNOTES

1. VASARI, Sansoni's edition, II, p. 520.

2. BUCKHARDT und BODE, *Cicerone*.

3.*Storia della Pittura*, II, p. 360.

4. Guido was Fra Angelico's baptismal name in the world.

5. MARCHESE, *Memorie dei più insigni pittori, scultori e architetti domenicani*, I, p. 267.

6. Bologna, Romagnoli 1878.

7. CAVALCASELLE, *Storia della Pittura*, II, p. 234.

8. VASARI, *Vita di Masaccio*, II, p. 299.

9. Museo civico. Sala 6, n. 7.

10. CARTIER, *Vie de Fra Angelico*. Paris, 1857, p. 356.

11. VASARI, II, p. 518.

12. VASARI, II, p. 528, note i. The translations from Vasari are from Bohn's edition.

13. Ibid., II, p. 528.

14. VASARI, II, p. 505.

15. VASARI, vol. II, p. 512.
Translation:

I raise my eyes, sweet Mary I behold,
With book in hand; an angel form is near.

It is the shining angel Gabriel
Who kneels before her in humility,
And saith: "Fear not, pure Virgin, I from heaven
A messenger from God omnipotent
Come down to bring glad tidings unto thee,

For he hath chosen thee for his blest spouse."

He saith again: "In heaven it is decreed
Thou shalt be mother of the Son of God,
Therefore the Father me, his angel, sends
To swift fulfil his sacred will and law.
And down from him the highest Lord to bring
This benediction unto which thou'rt called."

The angel's heaven-sent words were so inflamed
With sacred love's own virtue did they burn
They truly seemed to fall from God above.
With holy joy her beating heart was full:
"Behold," she said, "the handmaid of the Lord,
Be it to me according to his word."

But as she sat within her archèd cell
She wondered greatly how this thing should be:
"For I know not, nor speak with any man,"
To Gabriel she timidly responds.
Then quoth he: "Mary Hail! thou favoured art,
And full of grace, the Lord is with thee now."

And then came down the spirit of the Lord,
A ray of golden light shone round about,
It pierced her breast, that fruitful heaven-sent ray,
And from her womb, whose virgin purity
Was still inviolate, was born the Christ
While she a mother, was pure Virgin still.

Oh! lovers true, come hither unto her:
Madonna she of grace and beauty fair,
The earth and air but live for her sweet sake,
The queen of heaven, and pillar of the world:
He who would see the lovely damosel
One this Annunciation he should gaze.

16. From an anonymous "Laud" reprinted by GALLETTI, n.
CCLXVIII, p. 121.
17. Op. cit., I, p. 293.
18. *Vie de Fra Angelico*, p. 243.

19. Year 1894, p. 370.

20. Vol. II, p. 510.

21. Vol. I, p. 297.

22. VASARI, II, p. 510, note 1.

23. *Pictures in the National Gallery*, with descriptive text written by C. L. EASTLAKE. No. I, p. 10.

24. VASARI, II, p. 510.

25. This valuable painting was ceded by the monks of the "Scalzi" to the Museum of Madrid in 1861 at the suggestion of Señor Don Federigo de Madrazo. – *Catalogue of the Museum of Prado*, DON PEDRO DE MADRAZO 1889, p. 19.

26. VASARI, II, p. 510 and 511.

27. MÜNTZ, *Histoire de l'art pendant la Renaissance – Les Primitifs –* p. 653 and 658.

28. Op. cit., I, p. 308.

29. *La Sculpture Florentine*, Alinari, 1897, p. 152.

30. VASARI, II, p. 515.

31. *Par.*, Canto XXXI (CAREY'S translation).

32. *Par.*, Canto XXX (CAREY'S translation).

33. The *caròla* was a kind of sacred dance, in which the dancers holding hands move in a circle, singing as they go. It was supposed to be the dance of Paradise. – (*Translator's note.*)
Translation:
In Paradise that garden lies
Where love divine eternal shines,
And holy Saints *carolas* weave,
Their souls inflamed with sacred love.

The Saints in that bright joyous ring,
With Angels fair of all degrees,
Before the Bridegroom graceful move
And weave the dance of sacred love.

Those heavenly courts are full of grace,
With love immeasurable filled,
All in the dance angelic move
Inspired by their sweet Saviour's love.

Their robes of linen pure are made,
White, roseate, and of mingled hues;
Fair garlands on their heads they wear,

Fit crowns to crown them priests of love.

No head is there ungarlanded,
And youthful beams each joyous face;
In that bright court refreshed they move
Where everything o'erflows with love.

The garlands made of blossoms fair,
Shine brighter than the purest gold,
The pearly daisies glisten there
Emblazoning the heavenly love.

34. VENTURI, *Le Gallerie Italiane. La Galleria Nazionale di Roma*, vol. II, p. 89.

35. See *Gazette de Beaux Arts*, 1888. W. BODE, *La Renaissance au Musée de Berlin*; IV. *Les Peintres Florentins du XVme siècle*, p. 473.

36. CAVALCASELLE, *Storia della Pittura*, II, p. 369, note 2. Venturi thinks that the picture approaches more to the art of Gentile da Fabriano. See VASARI, *Gentile da Fabriano e Pisanello*. Firenze, Sansoni, 1897, p. x.

37. VASARI, II, *Vita di Michelozzo*, p. 440.

38. RICHA, *Le Chiese Fiorentine*, VII, p. 117.

39. Vol. II, p. 440. In October 1438 the monks demanded a subsidy to rebuild the dormitory which had been destroyed by fire. GAYE, I, p. 553.

40. Vol. II, p. 441. Some chroniclers attribute the design of the convent to Brunelleschi, and the direction and execution of the work to Michelozzi. The building was probably completed in 1443.

41. VASARI, II, p. 441.

42. Vol. II, p. 508.

43. *Katalog der Gemälde-Sammlung der kgl. älteren Pinakothek in München*. Mit einer historischen Einleitung von Dr. FRANZ VON REBER.

44. Vol. II, p. 507.

45. See VASARI, II, p. 508, and MARCHESE, op. cit., I, p. 326 and following.

46. MARCHESE, *San Marco illustrato*, p. 40.

47. RIO, op. cit., II. p. 314.

48. CARTIER, *Vie de Fra Angelico*, p. 231.

49. VASARI, II, p. 511.

50. MARCHESE, op. cit., I, p. 295.

51. *Il Santuario della SS. Annunziata di Firenze*, Guida storica illustrativa, compilata da un religioso dei servi di Maria. Firenze, Ricci, 1876, p. 87.

52. VASARI, II, p. 531, note 2.

53. RIO, *De l'art chrétien*, p. 368. "Michelozzo paraît avoir, dans ce tableau, de quarante-cinq à cinquante ans. Or, on suppose qu'il était né vers 1396, ce qui placerait l'exécution de ce tableau très-peu de temps avant le départ de l'artiste pour Rome, en 1445," p. 312, note I.

54. RIO, op. cit., II, p. 318 et seq.

55. RIO, op. cit, II, p. 315.

56. RICHA, *Le Chiese Fiorentine*, X, pp. 137-138.

57. VASARI, II, p. 516.

58. VASARI, II, p. 517.

59. VASARI, II, p. 517.

60. LUIGI FUMI, *Il duomo d'Orvieto e i suoi restauri*. Roma, Tipografia Cooperativa, p. 370.

61. *Storia della Pittura Italiana*, III, p. 83.

62. MÜNTZ, *Les Arts à la cour des Papes*. Première partie, p. 92.

63. PÉRATÉ, *Les Papes et les Arts*. Paris, Didot, 1895, p. 72. MÜNTZ, *Histoire de l'Art pendant la Renaissance*, I, p. 664, and M. FAUCON, *L'[OE]uvre de Fra Angelico à Rome* in the Newspaper *L'Art*, 1883, XXXV, pp. 141-147 and 167-175.

64. CROWE and CAVALCASELLE, *A new history of painting in Italy*. London, Murray, 1864, II, p. 500.

BIBLIOGRAPHY[1]

I   *Fra Angelico*

C. Argan: *Fra Angelico*, Skira, Geneva 1955

U. Baldini: *Beato Angelico*, Edizioni d'Arte il Fiorino, Florence 1986

L. Berti et al: *Angelico at San Marco*, Sansoni, Florence 1965

M. OskovitsL "La fase tarda del Beato Angelico", *Arte cristiana*, LXXI, 1983, 11-24

— "Arte e formazione religosa – Il caso del Beato Angelico", in *L'uomo di fronte all'arte. Valori estetici e valori etico-religiosi*, La Spezia, 1985, *Vita e Pensiero*, 1986, 153-164

P. Cardile: "Fra Angelico's Shop at San Domenico in Fiesole", Ph. D thesis, Yale University 1974

G. Didi-Huberman: *Fra Angelico. Dissemblance et Figuration*, Flammarion, Paris 1990

— "La dissemblance des figures selon Fra Angelico", *Mélanges de l'Ecole Française de Rome. Moyn Age – Temps Moderne*, XCVIII, 1986, 709-802

D. Dini & G. Bonsanti: "Fra Angelico e gli affreschi nel Convento di San Marco (ca. 1441-50)", in E. Borsook & F. Superbi Gioffredi, ed: *Tecnica e Stile. Esempi di pittura murale del Rinascimento italiano*, Harvard Center for Italian Renaissance Studies at Villa I Tatti, 1986, 17-24

A. Francini Ciaranfi: *Beato Angelico: Gli affreschi di San Marco*, Amilcare Pizzi S. p. A, Milan 1940

C. Gilbert: "A Sign about Signing in a Fresco by Fra Angelico", in *Tribute to Lotte Brand Phi;lip*, Abaris Books, New York 1985, 65-70

— "Fra Angeloc", *Theologische Realenzyklopädie*, II, 5, Waler de Gruyter, Berlin, 19978, 710-3

---

1 From *Fra Angelico* by Rosalind Mutter, Crescent Moon, 2008.

—"The Conversion of Fra Angelico", in *Scritti di Storia dell'Arte in onore di Roberto Salvini*, ed. C. De Benedictis, G.C. Sansoni Editore Nuova, Florence 1984, 281-7

A. Hertz: *Fra Angelico*, Edizioni Paoline, Rome 1983

William Hood: *Fra Angelico at San Marco*, Yale University Press, New Haven 1993

—"Fra Angelico at San Marco: Art and the Liturgy of Cloistered Life", in T. Verdon & J. Henderson, eds: *Christianity and the Renaissance*, Syracuse University Press, Syracuse 1990, 108-131

—"St Dominic's Manners of Praying: Gestures in Fra Angelico's Frescoes at S. Marco", *Art bulletin*, LXVIII, 1986, 195-206

P. Joannides: "Fra Angelico: Two Annunciations", *Arte cristiana*, LXXVII, 1989, 303-308

R. Krautheimer: "Fra Angelico and – perhaps – Alberti", in J. Plummer & I. Lavin, eds: *Studies in Late Medieval and Renaissance Painting Presented to Millard Meiss*, New York University Press, New York 1977, 290-296

A. Ladis: "Fra Angelico: newly discovered document from the 1420s", *Mitteilungen des Kunsthistorischen Institutes in Florenz*, XXV, 1981, 378-9

Christopher Lloyd: *Fra Angelico*, Phaidon 1979

S. Madigan: "A New Interpretation of the Iconography of Fra Angelico: Rosarian Organization in the Frescoed Cells of San Marco", MACAA paper, Hamlite University, St Paul, 1977

J. Miller: "Medici Patronage and the Iconography of Fra Angelico's San Marco Altarpiece", *Studies in Iconography*, XI, 1987, 1-13

S. Orlandi: *Beato Angelico*, Leo S. Olscki, Florence 1964

John Pope-Hennessy: *Fra Angelico*, Phaidon 1974

U. Procacci: "Recent restoration in Florence, II: Fra Angelico, Sassetta and others", *Burlington Magazine*, LXXXIX, 1947, 330-4

M. Salmi: *Beato Angelico*, Edizioni Valori Plastici, Rome 1958

P. Sheaffer: "White Light and Meditation at San Marco", *Memorie Domenicane*, XIV, 1983, 329-334

I. Strunk: *Fra Angelico aus dem Dominikanerorden*, B. Kuehlens Kunstanstalt u. Verlag, Gladbach 1916

C.G. Argan: *The Renaissance*, Thames & Hudson 1969

Karen Armstrong: *The Gospel According to Woman; Christianity's Creation of the Sex War in the West*, Pan 1987

Karen Arthurs: *A Survey of the Notions Behind, and the Mechanics of, Harmony Within the Composition of Art From Prehistory to the Renaissance*, BA thesis, Newcastle Polytechnic 1984

Geoffrey Ashe: *The Virgin: Mary's Cult and the Re-emergence of the Goddess*, Arkana 1987

—*Discovering the Goddess: A Personal Testimony*, Crescent Moon 1995

Michael Baxandall: *Painting and Experience in 15th Century Italy*, Oxford University Press 1988

—*Patterns of Intention: On the Historical Explanation of Pictures*, Yale University Press 1985

James Beck: *Italian Renaissance Painting*, Harper & Row, New York 1981

Ean Begg: *The Cult of the Black Virgin*, Routledge 1985

Bernard Berenson: *The Italian Painters of the Renaissance*, Phaidon 1952

—*Looking at Pictures with Bernard Berenson*, selected by Hann Kiel, Abrahams, New York 1974

Pamela Berger: *The Goddess Obscured*, Robert Hale 1988

Bruce Bernard: *The Queen of Heaven: A Selection of Painting the Virgin from the Twelfth to the Eighteenth Centuries*, Macdonald/ Orbis 1987

—*The Bible and Its Painters*, Orbis 1983

Botticelli: *The Complete Paintings of Botticelli*, Granada 1980

Charles Bouleau: *The Painter's Secret Geometry: A Study of Composition in Art*, tr Jonathan Griffin, Thames & Hudson 1963

Serge Bramly: *Leonardo: The Artist and the Man*, Michael Joseph 1992

Allan Brahama: *Italian Renaissance Painters of the Sixteenth Century*, National Gallery 1985

Helmut Brinker: *Zen in the Art of Painting*, Routledge & Kegan Paul 1987

Stephanie Brown: *Religious Painting*, Phaidon 1979

Jacob Burckhardt: *The Altarpiece in Renaissance Italy*, Phaidon 1988

Titus Burckhardt: *Sacred Art in East and West*, Perennial Book, Middlesex 1967

Ritchie Calder: *Leonardo and The Age of the Eye*, Heinemann 1970

Joseph Campbell: *The Power of Myth*, with Bill Moyers, ed. Betty Sue Flowers, Doubleday, New York 1988

Michael P. Carroll: *The Cult of the Virgin Mary*, Princeton University

Press, New Jersey 1986

Richard Cavendish: *Visions of Heaven and Hell*, Orbis 1977

Andre Chastel: *Art of the Italian Renaissance*, tr Peter & Linda Murray, Alpine Fine Arts Collection 1985

— *The Studios and Styles of the Renaissance, Italy 1460-1500*, tr Griffin, Thames & Hudson 1966

Herschel B. Chipp, ed. *Theories of Modern Art*, University Press of California, Los Angeles 1968

Bruce Cole: *The Renaissance Artist at Work*, John Murray 1983

Charles D. Cuttler: *Northern Painting From Pucelle to Bruegel*, Holt, Rineheart & Winston, New York 1968

Lene Dresen-Coenders, ed: *Saints and She-Devils: Images of Women in the 15th and 16th Centuries*, Rubicon Press 1987

Steven C. Dubin: *Arresting Images: Impolitic Art and Uncivil Actions*, Routledge 1992

Andrea Dworkin: *Intercourse*, Arrow 1988

— *Pornography: Men Possessing Women*, Women's Press 1984

Donald Ehresmann: "Some Observations on the Role of the Liturgy in the Early Winged Altarpiece", *Art Bulletin*, LXIV, 1982

Colin Eisler: *Early Netherlandish Painting: The Thyssen-Bornemisza Collection*, Sotheby's Publications 1989

Mircea Eliade: *Ordeal by Labyrinth*, University of Chicago Press 1984

— *Symbolism, the Sacred and the Arts*, Crossroad, New York 1985

Joan Evans, ed: *The Flowering of the Middle Ages*, Thames & Hudson 1966

Giorgio T. Faggin: *The Complete Paintings of the Van Eycks*, Wiedenfeld & Nicolson 1970

John Fletcher & Andrew Benjamin, ed; *Abjection, Melancholia and Love: the Work of Julia Kristeva*, Routledge 1990

S.J. Freedberg: *Painting of the High Renaissance in Rome and Florence*, Harper & Row, New York 1972

Sigmund Freud: *Leonardo da Vinci*, tr Alan Tyson, Penguin 1963

Max J. Friedlander: *From Van Eyck to Bruegel*, Phaidon 1969

— *The van Eycks, Petrus Christus*, Early Netherlandish Painting vol. 1, tr Heinz Norden, Sijthoff, Leyden, Netherlands 1967

Eugène Fromentin: *The Masters of Past Time: Dutch and Flemish Painting from Van Eyck to Rembrandt*, Phaidon 1981

Niny Garavaghlia: *The Complete Paintings of Mantegna*, Weidenfeld & Nicholson 1971

Fred Gettings: *The Hidden Art: A Study of the Occult Symbolism in Art*, Studio Vista 1978

Matila Ghyka: *The Geometry of Art and Life*, Sheed & Ward, New York

1946

Marija Gimbutas: *The Language of the Goddess*, Thames & Hudson 1989

Rona Goffen: *Giovanni Bellini*, Yale University Press, New Haven 1989

Robert Goldwater & Marco Treves, eds. *Artists on Art*, John Murray 1975

E.H. Gombrich: *Norm and Form: Studies in the Renaissance I*, Phaidon 1985

— *Symbolic Images, Renaissance Studies II*, Phaidon 1985

Cecil Gould: *Leonardo: The Artist and the Non-Artist*, Weidenfeld & Nicholson 1975

— "On the Direction of Light in Italian Renaissance Frescoes and Altarpieces", *Gazette des Beaux-Arts*, 6, XCVII, 1981

John Hale: *Italian Renaissance Painting*, Phaidon 1977

James Hall: *A Dictionary of Subjects and Symbols in Art*, John Murray 1984

Frederick Hartt: *History of Italian Renaissance Art: Painting, Sculpture, Architecture*, Thomas & Hudson 1987

— *Sandro Botticelli*, Collins 1954

P. Jolly: "Rogier van der Weyden's Escorial and Philadelphia *Crucifixions* and their relation to Fra Angelico at San Marco", *Oud Holland*, XCV, 1981, 113-126

Julia Kristeva: *The Kristeva Reader*, ed Toril Moi, Blackwell 1986

— *Desire in Language: A Semiotic Approach to Literature and Art*, ed Leon Roudiez, tr Thomas Gora, Alice Jardine & Leon Roudiez, Blackwell 1982

Weston La Barre: *The Ghost Dance*, Allen & Unwin 1972

Barbara Lane: *The Altar and the Altarpiece: Sacramental Themes in Early Netherlandish Painting*, New York 1984

— "Sacred vs Profane in Early Netherlandish Painting", *Simiolus*, XVIII, 1988

Leonardo da Vinci: *The Drawings of Leonardo da Vinci*, introduction A.E. Popham, Cape, 1964

— *Selections from the Notebooks*, Oxford University Press 1952

Michael Levey: *High Renaissance*, Penguin 1975

— *Early Renaissance*, Penguin 1967

Robert Longhi: *Piero della Francesca*, Milan 1955

Emile Male: *The Gothic Image*, Collins 1961

Elaine Marks & Isabelle de Courtivron, eds: *New French Feminisms: an Anthology*, Harvester Wheatsheaf 1981

G. Marchini: *Filippo Lippi*, Electa Editrice, Milan 1975

James Marrow: "Symbol and Meaning in Northern European Art of the Late Middle Ages and Early Renaissance", *Simiolus*, XVI, 1986

Milliard Meiss: "Light as Form and Symbol in Some Fifteenth Century Paintings", *Art Bulletin*, XXVII, 1945

J.C.J. Metford: *Dictionary of Christian Lore and Legend*, Thames & Hudson 1983

Edward Mullins: *The Painted Witch: Female Body, Male Art*, Secker & Warburg 1985

Peter & Linda Murray: *The Penguin Dictionary of Art and Artists*, Penguin 1976

Linda Murray: *High Renaissance*, Thames & Hudson 1977

Lynda Nead: *Female Nude: Art, Obscenity and Sexuality*, Routledge 1992

Erich Neumann: *The Great Mother*, Princeton University Press, New Jersey 1972

Shirley Nicholson, ed. *The Goddess Re-awakening: The Goddess Principle Today* Theosophical Publishing House, New York 1989

Rudolf Otto: *The Idea of the Holy*, Oxford University Press 1958

Erwin Panofsky: *Studies in Iconology*, Harper & Row, New York 1972

— *Early Netherlandish Painting*, Harvard University Press, Mass., 1953

Walter Pater: *The Renaissance*, Oxford University Press 1980

Michael Payne: *Reading Theory: An Introduction to Lacan, Derrida, and Kristeva*, Blackwell 1993

Robert Payne: *Leonardo da Vinci*, Robert hale 1979

Lotte Brand Philip: *The Ghent Altarpiece and the Art of Jan van Eyck*, Princeton University Press 1971

C. Purtle: *The Marian Paintings of Jan van Eyck*, Princeton University Press, Princeton 1982

Kathleen J. Reiger, ed: *The Spiritual Image in Modern Art*, Theosophical Publ-ishing House, Wheaton, Illinois 1987

D. Robb: "The Iconography of the Annunciation in the Fourteenth and Fifteenth Centuries", *Art Bulletin*, XVIII, 1936, 480-526

John Ruskin: *Works*, ed. E.T.Cook & A. Wedderburn, 39 vols, Allen 1903-12

Monica Sjöo & Barbara Mor: *The Great Cosmic Mother*, Harper & Row, San Francisco 1987

Alistair Smith: *Early Netherlandish and German Painting*, National Gallery 1985

J. Spencer: "Spatial Imagery of the Annunciation in Fifteenth-century Flor-ence", *Art Bulletin*, XXXVI, 1955, 273-280

Oswald Spengler: *The Decline of the West*, Allen & Unwin 1961

Wolfgang Stechow: *Northern Renaissance Art, 1400-1600, Sources and Documents*, Prentice-Hall, New Jersey 1966

L. Steinberg & S. Edgerton: "How shall this be? Reflections on Filippo Lippi's *Annunciation* in London", *Artibus et Historiæ*, VIII, 1987, 25-53

Victor I. Stoichita: *Leonardo da Vinci*, Abbey Library 1978

Nicholas Usherwood: *The Bible in 20th Century Art*, Pagoda Books 1987

Lionello Venturi: *Renaissance Painting, from Leonardo to Dürer*, Skira/Macmillan 1979

— *Italian Paintings*, Zwemmer 1950

— *Botticelli*, Phaidon 1964

Marina Warner: *Alone Of All Her Sex: The Myth and Cult of the Virgin Mary*, Picador 1985

— *Monuments and Maidens*, Weidenfeld & Nicholson 1985

Margaret Whinney: *Early Flemish Painters*, Faber 1966

John White: *The Birth and Rebirth of Pictorial Space*, Faber 1957/87

Peter Lamborn Wilson: *Angels*, Thames & Hudson 1980

Heinrich Wolfflin: *Classic Art*, Phaidon 1952/80

Marion Woodman: *The Pregnant Virgin: A Process of Psychological Transformation*, Inner City Books, Toronto 1989

Manfred Wudram: *Art of the Renaissance*, Weidenfeld & Nicolson 1985

J.E. Zeigler: "The Medieval Virgin as Object: Art of Anthropology?", *Historical Reflections*, XVI, 1989

Charles Zika: "Hosts, Processions and Pilgrimages: Controlling the Sacred in Fifteenth-Century Germany", *Past and Present*, CXVIII, 1988

CRESCENT MOON PUBLISHING

web: www.crmoon.com e-mail: cresmopub@yahoo.co.uk

ARTS, PAINTING, SCULPTURE

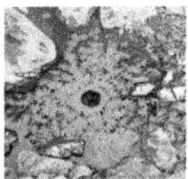

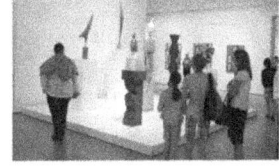

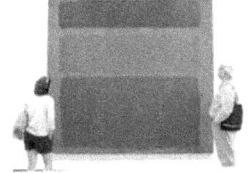

The Art of Andy Goldsworthy
Andy Goldsworthy: Touching Nature
Andy Goldsworthy in Close-Up
Andy Goldsworthy: Pocket Guide
Andy Goldsworthy In America
Land Art: A Complete Guide
The Art of Richard Long
Richard Long: Pocket Guide
Land Art In the UK
Land Art in Close-Up
Land Art In the U.S.A.
Land Art: Pocket Guide
Installation Art in Close-Up
Minimal Art and Artists In the 1960s and After
Colourfield Painting
Land Art DVD, TV documentary
Andy Goldsworthy DVD, TV documentary
The Erotic Object: Sexuality in Sculpture From Prehistory to the Present Day
Sex in Art: Pornography and Pleasure in Painting and Sculpture
Postwar Art
Sacred Gardens: The Garden in Myth, Religion and Art
Glorification: Religious Abstraction in Renaissance and 20th Century Art
Early Netherlandish Painting
Leonardo da Vinci
Piero della Francesca
Giovanni Bellini
Fra Angelico: Art and Religion in the Renaissance
Mark Rothko: The Art of Transcendence
Frank Stella: American Abstract Artist
Jasper Johns
Brice Marden
Alison Wilding: The Embrace of Sculpture
Vincent van Gogh: Visionary Landscapes
Eric Gill: Nuptials of God
Constantin Brancusi: Sculpting the Essence of Things
Max Beckmann
Caravaggio
Gustave Moreau
Egon Schiele: Sex and Death In Purple Stockings
Delizioso Fotografico Fervore: Works In Process 1
Sacro Cuore: Works In Process 2
The Light Eternal: J.M.W. Turner
The Madonna Glorified: Karen Arthurs

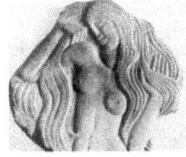

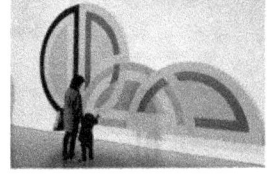

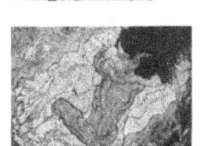

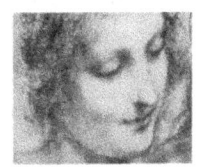

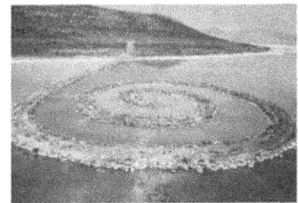

LITERATURE

J.R.R. Tolkien: The Books, The Films, The Whole Cultural Phenomenon
J.R.R. Tolkien: Pocket Guide
Tolkien's Heroic Quest
The *Earthsea* Books of Ursula Le Guin
Beauties, Beasts and Enchantment: Classic French Fairy Tales
German Popular Stories by the Brothers Grimm
Philip Pullman and *His Dark Materials*
Sexing Hardy: Thomas Hardy and Feminism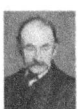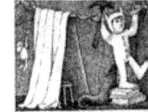
Thomas Hardy's *Tess of the d'Urbervilles*
Thomas Hardy's *Jude the Obscure*
Thomas Hardy: The Tragic Novels
Love and Tragedy: Thomas Hardy
The Poetry of Landscape in Hardy
Wessex Revisited: Thomas Hardy and John Cowper Powys
Wolfgang Iser: Essays and Interviews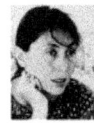
Petrarch, Dante and the Troubadours
Maurice Sendak and the Art of Children's Book Illustration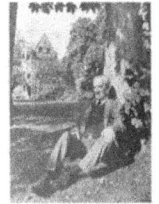
Andrea Dworkin
Cixous, Irigaray, Kristeva: The *Jouissance* of French Feminism
Julia Kristeva: Art, Love, Melancholy, Philosophy, Semiotics and Psychoanalysis
Hélène Cixous I Love You: The *Jouissance* of Writing
Luce Irigaray: Lips, Kissing, and the Politics of Sexual Difference
Peter Redgrove: Here Comes the Flood
Peter Redgrove: Sex-Magic-Poetry-Cornwall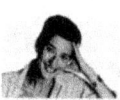
Lawrence Durrell: Between Love and Death, East and West
Love, Culture & Poetry: Lawrence Durrell
Cavafy: Anatomy of a Soul
German Romantic Poetry: Goethe, Novalis, Heine, Hölderlin
Feminism and Shakespeare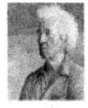
Shakespeare: Love, Poetry & Magic
The Passion of D.H. Lawrence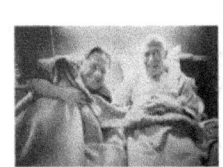
D.H. Lawrence: Symbolic Landscapes
D.H. Lawrence: Infinite Sensual Violence
Rimbaud: Arthur Rimbaud and the Magic of Poetry
The Ecstasies of John Cowper Powys
Sensualism and Mythology: The Wessex Novels of John Cowper Powys
Amorous Life: John Cowper Powys and the Manifestation of Affectivity (H.W. Fawkner)
Postmodern Powys: New Essays on John Cowper Powys (Joe Boulter)
Rethinking Powys: Critical Essays on John Cowper Powys
Paul Bowles & Bernardo Bertolucci
Rainer Maria Rilke
Joseph Conrad: *Heart of Darkness*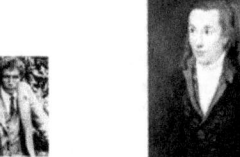
In the Dim Void: Samuel Beckett
Samuel Beckett Goes into the Silence
André Gide: Fiction and Fervour
Jackie Collins and the Blockbuster Novel
Blinded By Her Light: The Love-Poetry of Robert Graves
The Passion of Colours: Travels In Mediterranean Lands
Poetic Forms

POETRY

Ursula Le Guin: Walking In Cornwall
Peter Redgrove: Here Comes The Flood
Peter Redgrove: Sex-Magic-Poetry-Cornwall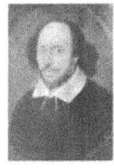
Dante: Selections From the Vita Nuova
Petrarch, Dante and the Troubadours
William Shakespeare: Sonnets
William Shakespeare: Complete Poems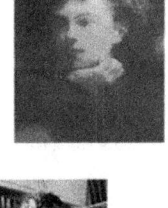
Blinded By Her Light: The Love-Poetry of Robert Graves
Emily Dickinson: Selected Poems
Emily Brontë: Poems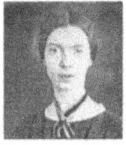
Thomas Hardy: Selected Poems
Percy Bysshe Shelley: Poems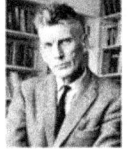
John Keats: Selected Poems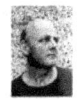
Joh n Keats: Poems of 1820
D.H. Lawrence: Selected Poems
Edmund Spenser: Poems
Edmund Spenser: Amoretti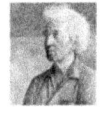
John Donne: Poems
Henry Vaughan: Poems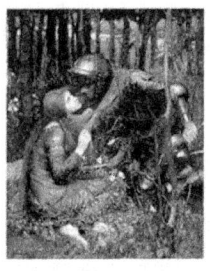
Sir Thomas Wyatt: Poems
Robert Herrick: Selected Poems
Rilke: Space, Essence and Angels in the Poetry of Rainer Maria Rilke
Rainer Maria Rilke: Selected Poems
Friedrich Hölderlin: Selected Poems
Arseny Tarkovsky: Selected Poems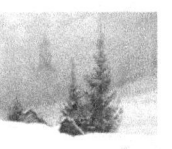
Arthur Rimbaud: Selected Poems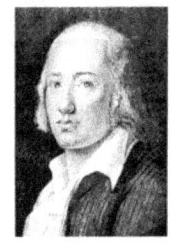
Arthur Rimbaud: A Season in Hell
Arthur Rimbaud and the Magic of Poetry
Novalis: Hymns To the Night
German Romantic Poetry
Paul Verlaine: Selected Poems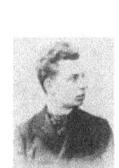
Elizaethan Sonnet Cycles
D.J. Enright: By-Blows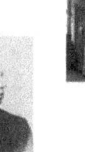
Jeremy Reed: Brigitte's Blue Heart
Jeremy Reed: Claudia Schiffer's Red Shoes
Gorgeous Little Orpheus
Radiance: New Poems
Crescent Moon Book of Nature Poetry
Crescent Moon Book of Love Poetry
Crescent Moon Book of Mystical Poetry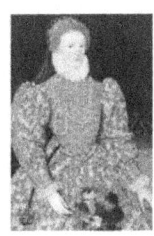
Crescent Moon Book of Elizabethan Love Poetry
Crescent Moon Book of Metaphysical Poetry
Crescent Moon Book of Romantic Poetry
Pagan America: New American Poetry

MEDIA, CINEMA, FEMINISM and CULTURAL STUDIES

J.R.R. Tolkien: The Books, The Films, The Whole Cultural Phenomenon
J.R.R. Tolkien: Pocket Guide
The *Lord of the Rings* Movies: Pocket Guide
The Cinema of Hayao Miyazaki
Hayao Miyazaki: *Princess Mononoke*: Pocket Movie Guide
Hayao Miyazaki: *Spirited Away*: Pocket Movie Guide
Tim Burton : Hallowe'en For Hollywood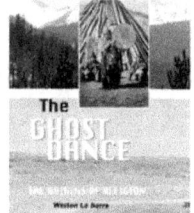
Ken Russell
Ken Russell: *Tommy*: Pocket Movie Guide
The Ghost Dance: The Origins of Religion
The Peyote Cult
Cixous, Irigaray, Kristeva: The *Jouissance* of French Feminism
Julia Kristeva: Art, Love, Melancholy, Philosophy, Semiotics and Psychoanalysis
Luce Irigaray: Lips, Kissing, and the Politics of Sexual Difference
Hélène Cixous I Love You: The *Jouissance* of Writing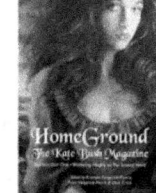
Andrea Dworkin
'Cosmo Woman': The World of Women's Magazines
Women in Pop Music
HomeGround: The Kate Bush Anthology
Discovering the Goddess (Geoffrey Ashe)
The Poetry of Cinema
The Sacred Cinema of Andrei Tarkovsky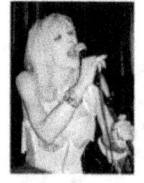
Andrei Tarkovsky: Pocket Guide
Andrei Tarkovsky: *Mirror*: Pocket Movie Guide
Andrei Tarkovsky: *The Sacrifice*: Pocket Movie Guide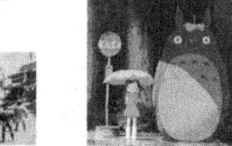
Walerian Borowczyk: Cinema of Erotic Dreams
Jean-Luc Godard: The Passion of Cinema
Jean-Luc Godard: *Hail Mary*: Pocket Movie Guide
Jean-Luc Godard: *Contempt*: Pocket Movie Guide
Jean-Luc Godard: *Pierrot le Fou*: Pocket Movie Guide
John Hughes and Eighties Cinema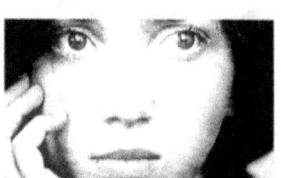
Ferris Bueller's Day Off: Pocket Movie Guide
Jean-Luc Godard: Pocket Guide
The Cinema of Richard Linklater
Liv Tyler: Star In Ascendance
Blade Runner and the Films of Philip K. Dick
Paul Bowles and Bernardo Bertolucci
Media Hell: Radio, TV and the Press
An Open Letter to the BBC
Detonation Britain: Nuclear War in the UK
Feminism and Shakespeare
Wild Zones: Pornography, Art and Feminism
Sex in Art: Pornography and Pleasure in Painting and Sculpture
Sexing Hardy: Thomas Hardy and Feminism

The Light Eternal is a model monograph, an exemplary job. The subject matter of the book is beautifully organised and dead on beam. (Lawrence Durrell)
It is amazing for me to see my work treated with such passion and respect. (Andrea Dworkin)

CRESCENT MOON PUBLISHING
P.O. Box 1312, Maidstone, Kent, ME14 5XU, Great Britain. www.crmoon.com

cresmopub@yahoo.co.uk   www.crescentmoon.org.uk